MICHELANGELO

Yvonne Paris

MICHELANGELO

1475–1564

translated by
Sophie Leighton

PaRragon

Bath · New York · Singapore · Hong Kong · Cologne · Delhi · Melbourne

CONTENTS

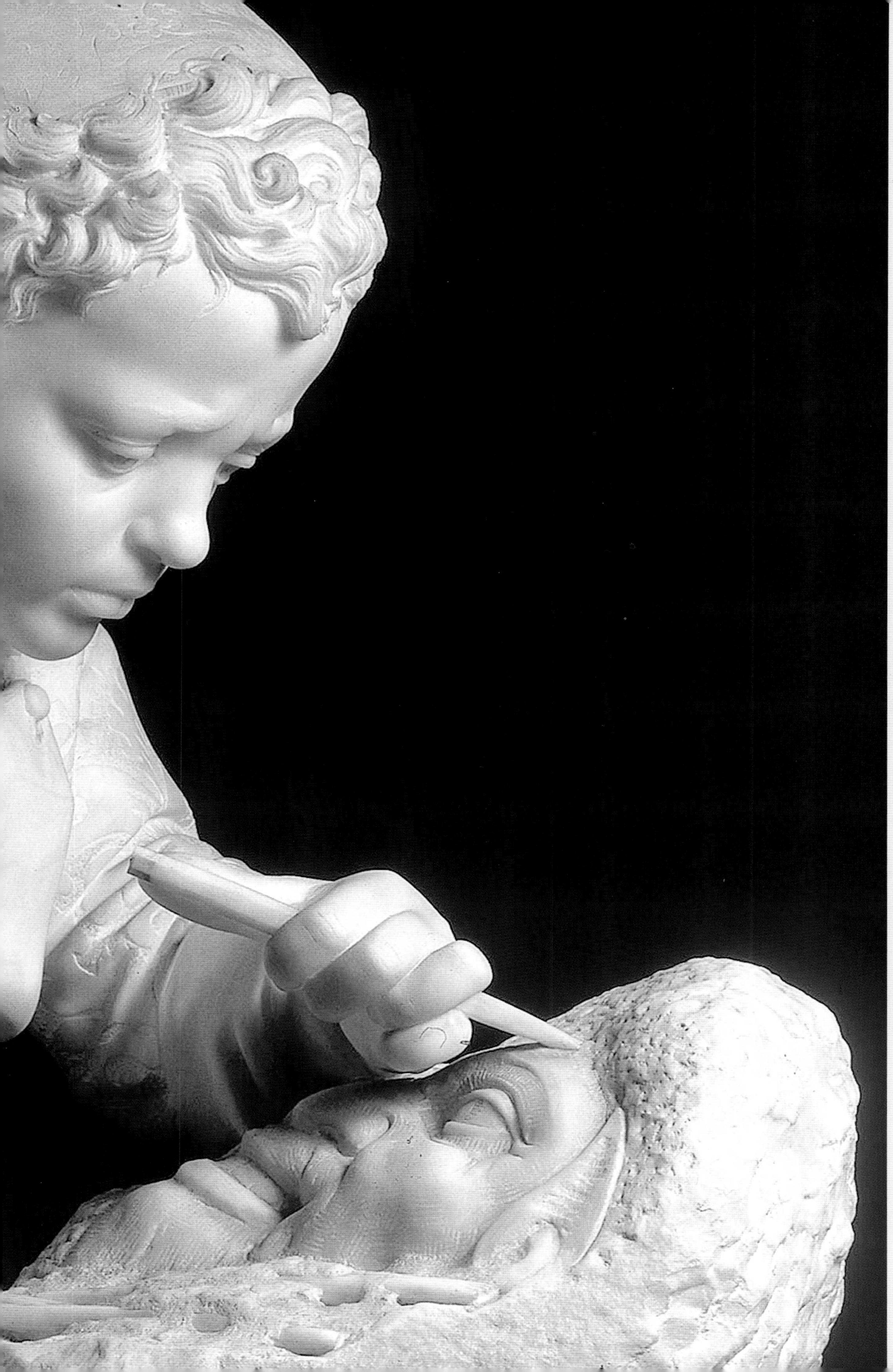

I. MICHELANGELO'S CHILDHOOD AND YOUTH

MICHELANGELO'S CHILDHOOD AND YOUTH

FROM THE CASENTINO VALLEY TO THE COURT OF LORENZO THE MAGNIFICENT

The last few days of April 1478 were a dark time in the history of Florence. The Signoria, the city government, fell within the principality of the Medici prince, Lorenzo the Magnificent, who on April 26 had narrowly escaped an enemy conspiracy in which his brother Giuliano was murdered by being stabbed to death during High Mass in the Cathedral of Santa Maria del Fiore. Lorenzo himself managed to escape with his wounds into the Sacristy and to save his life. A fearsome vengeance was unleashed on the rebels: "And that evening they hung Jacopo, son of Messr Poggio, from the windows of the Palagio de' Signori, and likewise the bishop of Pisa, and Franceschino de' Pazzi, naked; and about twenty men besides, some at the Palagio de' Signori, and others at the Palagio del Podestà and at the Casa del Capitano, all at the windows.... And that evening of the 28th [April 1478], about 23 in the evening, [7 p.m.], Messr Jacopo de' Pazzi and Renato de' Pazzi were hung at the windows of the Palagio de' Signori, over the *ringhiera*; and so many of their men with them, that during these three days the number of those killed amounted to more than seventy" (Landucci).

This is how the Florentine citizen Luca Landucci describes the vengeance visited on the Pazzi, the patrician family in rivalry with the Medici, and on their supporters, in his famous chronicle of events in Florence between 1450 and 1516, which is one of the most important historical sources for the Florentine Renaissance. The city had been seized by a genuine blood lust, and its streets were filled with the cry *"muoino e traditori"*:

◁ **Leonardo da Vinci,** *Bernardo Bandini Baroncelli, the Murderer of Giuliano de' Medici, Executed by Rope,* 1479.
Pen and Indian ink, 7½ x 3 in. (19.2 x 7.8 cm).
Musée Bonnat, Bayonne, France

▷ **Daniele da Volterra,** *Bust of Michelangelo* (detail), 1564–66.
Bronze. Bargello Museum, Florence.

PAGES 6–7
Emilio Zocchi, *The Boy Michelangelo Carving the Head of a Faun,* 1861.
Marble, 23½ in. (60 cm) high. Galleria Pitti, Sala delle Allegorie, Florence.

View of Florence, so-called chain-map, ca. 1470, Museo di Firenze Com'era, Florence, showing the old city north of the Arno and the circular wall surrounding it; in the city center appears the Cathedral with the cupola constructed by Filippo Brunelleschi.

death to the traitors. These events conjure up a vivid picture of the conditions that prevailed in Florence in the year that Michelangelo, as a three-year-old boy, arrived in his family's native city.

The second son of Ludovico Buonarroti, Michelangelo was born on March 6, 1475, in Caprese (today known as Caprese Michelangelo), a village near Arezzo in the Casentino valley. The Florentines initially recorded the year as 1474 because their calendar then recorded the first three months against

the preceding year. Michelangelo's father came from an old patrician Florentine family, the Buonarroti Simoni, whose members had held honorable public office since the middle of the fourteenth century. The Florentine records show that they belonged in the ranks of the XII Buonuomini (Twelve Good Men), as well as being members of the Gonfalioniere di Compagnia (Sovereign Magistrates) of the Santa Croce city district: One of their ancestors, Simone Buonarroti, had even been a member of the Consiglio dei Cento Savi (Council of the Hundred Wise

FIORENZA

Men). Michelangelo's mother Francesca also came from a highly regarded Florentine family, and was the daughter of Neri di Miniato del Sera and Bonda Rucellai. When Michelangelo was born, however, the illustrious days of the Buonarroti Simoni were long past; his father, a supporter of the pro-papal Guelf Party, held the office of *podestà* (chief magistrate) of Chiusi and Caprese, and had been called away from Florence for six months in this capacity. Although Michelangelo's father strove to do justice to his ancestors' fame, he remained a man who

was lacking in ambition or aspirations. Later, Michelangelo not only felt responsible for the family, for example, supporting his father with sums of money throughout his life; he also exerted his authority to establish his brothers in their positions, as his correspondence with them attests.

Michelangelo was baptized on March 8 in the church of San Giovanni in Caprese. At the end of the same month, his father's contract came to an end and the family moved back to Florence. Michelangelo, however, remained in nearby

Settignano, where he was given to a wet nurse. At that time, Settignano was a village of stonemasons in which *pietra serena*, the malleable gray sandstone typical of the area, was mined.

Michelangelo's wet nurse was married to a stonemason and Michelangelo later claimed that his propensity for sculpture dated back to those days since, along with his wet nurse's milk, he had "sucked in the chisels and hammer" that produced his figures.

In that same fateful year of 1478, Michelangelo arrived at his parents' town house in Florence. Of six children he was the second eldest after his brother Lionardo, who became a Dominican monk in 1490. In December 1481, when Michelangelo was six years old, his mother Francesca died. The identity of the mother of Matteo, the sixth child, remains uncertain; it seems likely that he was born of Ludovico's second marriage to Lucrezia degli Ubaldini, who had married Michelangelo's father in 1485. This marriage also ended early, with Lucrezia's death in 1497.

Different views have prevailed to this day about how the young Michelangelo came to pursue his training. Based primarily on the accounts of his biographers Giorgio Vasari and Ascanio Condivi, many authors relate that Michelangelo attended the grammar school of the Florentine humanist Francesco da Urbino around 1482 and had already revealed his artistic talent there. There is reference to his tireless drawing exercises, for which his friend Francesco Granacci (1469/70–1543, ill. p.12)—who was just a few years older and already working in the Ghirlandaio brothers' workshop in Florence—is thought to have supplied him with paper from the master Domenico Ghirlandaio. For these early endeavors, however, his father and tutor were said to have shown little understanding; to added anecdotal effect, Vasari reports that Michelangelo even received blows for this from time to time, but that the father finally capitulated to his son's irrepressible enthusiasm and accordingly sent Michelangelo to the famous workshop, the *bottega* (workshop) of Domenico and Davide Ghirlandaio, in 1488.

The more recent Michelangelo literature, according to the biography by Michelangelo expert Antonio Forcellino, provides a more objective picture, which takes closer account of the reality of the Buonarrotis' circumstances at that time. According to the family tradition, Michelangelo would have received a classical education, securing him a future as a banker or merchant. Yet Ludovico Buonarroti did not have the available means to give his son such an education. It was certainly no easy decision for him to send Michelangelo to learn a trade, which hardly befitted the rank of offspring of a patrician family, and would have entailed some loss of social status. In order to mitigate this stigma a little, the least his son could do would be to learn his trade in one of the best Florentine

workshops. The contract made between Ludovico Buonarroti and the Ghirlandaio brothers, dated April 1, 1488, attests the thirteen-year-old Michelangelo's admission to the Florentine master's highly reputable painting workshop for a three-year training period.

How quickly Michelangelo's extraordinary talent came to light, astonishing even his famous teacher Domenico Ghirlandaio (1449–94), is something that his biographers Vasari and Condivi never cease to emphasize. Both report an episode in the Ghirlandaio workshop in which Michelangelo is supposed to have had the audacity to improve a copy by the master and then to make fun of it. This led some authors to identify an arrogance already revealed in the young artist that prefigured his fearsome creative temperament, the *"terribilità,"* of later years. Views concerning the pupil's relationship with his teacher are, however, divided to this day. While some refer to the master's jealousy of his ambitious pupil, others regard this incident as having caused deep offense to Domenico, precipitating Michelangelo's departure from the Ghirlandaio workshop.

It is known for certain that Michelangelo learned the highly exacting fresco technique during his training with the Ghirlandaio brothers. During this period, the workshop was occupied with the fresco series in the Tornabuoni Chapel in the Florentine church of Santa Maria Novella (ill. p.13). The artists with whom Michelangelo was intensely concerned at that time included Giotto, Masaccio, and Donatello, as is documented by his early drawings (ill. pp.14–15). Copying older works was part of the training and was a prerequisite for learning the art of drawing. Michelangelo was able to study Masaccio's frescoes in the Florentine church of Santa Maria del Carmine and Giotto's wall paintings in the Peruzzi Chapel in Santa Croce.

Michelangelo's interest in plastic study emerges even in his early drawings: the expressive modeling of the figures and the masterly portrayal of the arrangement of folds in the garments already anticipate his sculptural genius. It is conceivable that, for the ambitious young artist, painting did not constitute the requisite challenge, and he recognized his stronger propensity for sculpture, which is why he prematurely ended the training period and left the Ghirlandaio workshop early at the end of

Domenico Ghirlandaio, *Birth of John the Baptist* (detail with ladies of the court and Lucrezia Tornabuoni), 1486–90.
Fresco. Santa Maria Novella, Tornabuoni Chapel, Florence.

Choir of Santa Maria Novella, Florence, interior view of the Tornabuoni Chapel with Domenico Ghirlandaio's frescoes.

◁ **Francesco Granacci**, *Charles VIII's Entry into Florence*, 1518.
Oil on wood, 29½ in x 48 in. (75 x 122 cm). Uffizi Gallery, Florence.

Masaccio, *Peter Distributes the Goods and Death of Ananias*,
ca. 1425–28. Fresco, 90½ x 63¾ in. (230 x 162 cm).
Santa Maria del Carmine, Brancacci Chapel, Florence.

Two figures after Giotto's fresco *John the Evangelist's Ascension into Heaven* in the Peruzzi Chapel in Santa Croce, Florence, ca. 1490. Pen and Indian ink in two colors on metal stylus, 12½ x 8 in. (31.6 x 20.4 cm). Musée du Louvre, Cabinet des Dessins, Paris.

the first year in 1489. According to Vasari, the master Domenico himself recommended his pupil Michelangelo, together with his friend Francesco Granacci, to the city ruler Lorenzo de' Medici as students for his sculpture garden at San Marco. Lorenzo, who is said to have complained that "he could find no great and noble sculptors to compare with the many contemporary painters of ability and repute," again according to Vasari, had asked the Florentine master to send young people from his workshop who showed a desire to sculpt "along to his garden, where they would be trained and formed in a manner that would do honor to himself, to Domenico, and to the whole city" (*Vasari*).

◁ *Group of Three Men Standing Facing Left* (thought to be copy of Masaccio's fresco *Sagra del Carmine*), ca. 1490.
Pen and Indian ink in two colors, 11½ x 8 in. (29.4 x 20.1 cm).
Graphische Sammlung Albertina, Vienna.

This early drawing by Michelangelo is considered one of the finest works of his youth. The highly differentiated composition of the figure in the foreground shows not only the young artist's outstanding drawing talent but also his interest in the plastic arts.

IN THE MEDICI SCULPTURE GARDEN

The Medici sculpture garden gained attention from the 1470s; it was situated on the Via Larga, between the San Marco monastery and the family's splendid palace, which had been built by Lorenzo de' Medici's grandfather Cosimo, "il Vecchio" (the old one). The inspiration for Lorenzo de' Medici's collection of what were mainly antique statues and fragments had come from the collecting passion of the Roman cardinals and high-ranking dignitaries whom he had known since his visit to the Eternal City in 1471 in the company of the famous architect and humanist Leon Battista Alberti. However, for him this was about much more than a mere accumulation of antique artworks. By inviting young artists and scholars there to study antiquity, he was able to prove himself a generous and

Florentine citizens such as Alamanno Rinuccini also spoke after Lorenzo's death of his tyranny; the Medici prince had "without regard to rules and law managed things entirely as he pleased and finally even planned to take over the republic like Julius Caesar.... Many people had known about his abuses of public funds, but no one had dared to speak out" (Walter). Yet despite every criticism of his rule, the service of Lorenzo the Magnificent is historically undisputed. The fostering of art and culture played a central role for him, since he also showed an unerring skill for identifying talent. He thus assembled at his court the most highly respected artists, writers, philosophers, and scholars of the day, who devoted themselves to the study and interpretation of models from antiquity (ill. pp.16, 25).

Lorenzo was quick to recognize Michelangelo's extraordinary talent and he became the young artist's most important patron. The annals of art history contain what is now a famous anecdote concerning an encounter between Lorenzo and Michelangelo in the garden of San Marco. Michelangelo was working on a faun's head (unpreserved) based on antique models (ill. p.17). When Lorenzo saw the work, he asked the young artist why he had allowed the faun so many teeth, since even a faun would lose its teeth in old age. Afterward, Michelangelo reached for his chisel and, according to Condivi, "removed an upper tooth from his old man, drilling the gum as if it had come out with the root, and the following day he awaited the Magnificent with eager longing" (Condivi). Lorenzo was evidently pleased by this and at the same time highly amused; the young artist had won his sympathy. As late as the nineteenth century, the incident provided the inspiration for a small marble sculpture by Emilio Zocchi that in a distinctly trivial way depicts Michelangelo, at just fifteen years old, chiseling his faun's bust (ill. pp.6–7).

Francesco Furini, *Lorenzo the Magnificent with the Philosophers and Poets in the Platonic Academy*, 1636. Fresco. Pitti Palace, Sala degli Argenti, Florence.

benevolent ruler. Fostering art and culture thus assumed an important role as part of the subtle strategy for dominance that Lorenzo developed following the Pazzi conspiracy of 1478.

This uprising against the Medici marked the culmination of the smoldering struggles for supremacy between the leading Florentine family clans. Lorenzo used this incident to dispose of his political opponents once and for all and to strengthen his claim to power. He set up a prince's court that made him to all intents and purposes an autocrat, although nominally Florence was still a republic. Lorenzo's credit for the unparalleled cultural and economic blossoming experienced by Florence under his patronage as a city ruler is uncontested. However, although Lorenzo entered history with the epithet "il Magnifico" (the Magnificent), his rule following the bloody conspiracy of 1478 bore tyrannical traits that he sought to conceal with great skill. But Lorenzo's exercise of power was drawing criticism even from contemporaries. It was not only the repentance-preacher Savonarola (1452–98) who described the prince as a cruel, violent, and avaricious ruler. Leading

Domenico Ghirlandaio, *Annunciation to Zeccharia* (detail), 1486–90. From the right: Gentile Becchi, Angelo Poliziano, Cristoforo Landino, Marsilio Ficino. Fresco. Santa Maria Novella, Tornabuoni Chapel, Florence.

Ottavio Vannini, *Michelangelo Presents his Faun's Head to Lorenzo de' Medici*, 1635.
Fresco. Pitti Palace, Sala degli Argenti, Florence.

The garden of San Lorenzo, however, also plays a role in Michelangelo's life because of an incident that was literally to scar him for his whole life. Vasari relates that another student, Pietro Torrigiani, who was jealous and envious of Lorenzo's preference for Michelangelo, dealt him such a powerful punch on the nose that Michelangelo's physiognomy was for ever characterized by a broken nose, as is clearly visible on all the portraits (ill. p.9). Torrigiani had to leave Florence in 1490 or 1491 because of his brutality.

Through Lorenzo's support, Michelangelo came to enjoy the benefits of a courtly education. At the Medici court, the foundations of his humanistic education were laid; he received the privilege of being allowed to study in a sculpture garden under the direction of Bertoldo di Giovanni (ca. 1420–91), a student of Donatello, and here his sculptural talent could develop. Here he also met a group of outstanding scholars whom Lorenzo gathered at his court: the humanist and man of letters Angelo Poliziano (1454–94), who was also tutor to Lorenzo's sons, the Plato and Plotinus translator Marsilio Ficino (1433–99), the Dante scholar Cristoforo Landino

(1424–98), and the philosopher Giovanni Pico della Mirandola (1463–94). The last interpreted the philosophies of Plato and Aristotle and exercised considerable influence on the development of Neoplatonism. The education that Michelangelo received here is also attested by the fact that a few years after Lorenzo's death, as a guest of the Bolognese nobleman Gianfrancesco Aldovrandi, Michelangelo read to him from the works of Dante, Petrarch, and Boccaccio, as reported by Vasari and Condivi. Furthermore, Michelangelo's poems also reveal the influence of Platonist and Neoplatonic ideas.

Again according to Condivi and Vasari, it was the above-mentioned humanist Angelo Poliziano who encouraged Michelangelo to create one of his earliest indisputably sculptural works. This was the sculptural transposition of one of Ovid's famous *Metamorphoses*, concerning the abduction of Hippodameia by the centaur, Eurytion, and the ensuing battle between lapiths and centaurs. Michelangelo represented the battle in a marble relief that he worked—*mezzo rilievo*—as a high relief in an extremely narrow space (ill. pp.18–19). He thereby made reference to antique reliefs that were well known in his

Bertoldo di Giovanni, *Battle Relief*, ca. 1475.
Bronze, 17 x 39 in. (43 x 99 cm). Bargello Museum, Florence.

◁ *Battle of the Centaurs*, ca. 1492.
Marble, 31½ x 35¾ in. (80 x 90.5 cm). Casa Buonarroti, Florence.

Michelangelo far surpassed the *Battle Relief* of his teacher Bertoldo di
Giovanni, for instance in the concentrated movement of the individual
figures and the lively composition of their nudity, as well as the clarity
and inner tension of the whole composition. He was evidently strongly
attached to this work of his youth—during his lifetime he never parted
with it.

time in Florence, such as from the drawings of the humanist
Ciriaco d'Ancona, which copied the ornamental sculpture of
the Parthenon Temple in Athens, including the metope relief
depicting battles between lapiths and centaurs.

While *Battle of the Centaurs*, originating around 1492,
already revealed a basic theme that would recur throughout
Michelangelo's artistic work—the portrayal of the human body
in motion—it also assumed a special position in Michelangelo's
work as the turning point that revealed the emergence of his
sculptural genius. This is due primarily to two revolutionary
innovations. Here the artist breaks away from the Florentine
tradition of relief depictions by Donatello or Lorenzo Ghiberti,
which are notable for their representation of events in distinct,
parallel, iconographic planes (ill. p.20). Michelangelo, by
contrast, works the figures in *Battle of the Centaurs* out of a
continuous spatial structure from which the naked bodies
organically emerge. This progressive treatment, in which the
representational planes leading from the relief background to
the surface are fused seamlessly together, generates a genuine
iconographic space in which the naked bodies take long strides
into the space in a perspectivally consistent way. Any narrative
embellishment has been omitted in favor of the concentration
on the battle action, in which the closely pressed bodies revolve
in a huge variety of movements around the warrior in the center
of the composition. The dynamism of the relief inspired the art
historian Ernst Benkard as recently as the 1930s to refer to the
"surging swell in marble."

If we consider the bodies of those who are fighting, here,
too, Michelangelo's supreme creative ability is revealed.
Connecting individual body parts presented huge challenges
to artists at that time in sculptural transposition; this mainly
involved "hanging" the limbs on to the joints, which often
looked very rigid and stiff in the sculptures. Michelangelo

Donatello, *Herod's Banquet*, ca. 1435.
Marble, 19¾ x 28 in. (50 x 71 cm). Musée des Beaux-Arts, Lille, France.

succeeded, however, in connecting the individual body parts so harmoniously through the joints that they appeared organically formed. An impressive example is the figure turning his upper body on the left side of the relief. At the same time, the figures show markedly individual features, so that for example, the bald old man lifting a stone at the left edge of the relief was identified as Phidias, whose features correspond to the Greek writer Plutarch's descriptions (ca. AD 46–120).

The programmatic status of *Battle of the Centaurs* is attested by the second major innovation, which manifests itself in the technical execution and is connected with the concept of "*non finito*," the unfinished or uncompleted artwork. It can clearly be observed from the relief that Michelangelo used every segment of the marble tablet: For example, instead of hollowing out the space behind the figures on the surface, he arranged more bodies here, which ultimately stand out only faintly from the relief background and simply appear uncompleted. It is known that Michelangelo deliberately worked with the various stages of non-completion. He was working from his *concetto*, the concept that the stone should impose itself on the artist—who only, as it were, reveals what the stone already conceals in itself. As Michelangelo himself expressed it: "The greatest artist does not have any concept that a single piece of marble does not itself contain within its excess." This *concetto* thus moved the immanent idea of the artwork, not its perfect execution, into the foreground.

How bold and progressive Michelangelo's relief of *Battle of the Centaurs* truly was is shown by a comparison with his slightly earlier relief, *Madonna of the Steps* (ill. p.21). Clearly visible on this low-relief, *rilievo schiaccato*, originating around 1490 to 1492, remains on the one hand his indebtedness to the representational principles of the fifteenth-century models, in particular Donatello, which also characterized the teaching of

Bertoldo di Giovanni in the Medici sculpture garden. On the other hand, the representation of the seated Madonna in profile with her abstract physiognomy contains some clear references to antique funeral steles. The young artist's connection with fifteenth-century Florentine tradition emerges above all in the construction of the iconographic space: It is subdivided by two parallel iconographic planes, the Madonna in the foreground, and the angel on the steps in the rear who are separated by the balusters on which the angel is leaning. Remarkable in the execution is the modeling of the bodies, if we consider, for example, the back and the arm of the baby Jesus or the forward-curving shoulder of the angel in the background.

Closer analysis reveals how far removed this votive relief remains from the technical virtuosity of *Battle of the Centaurs* by some imperfections in the execution. Clear indications of this are the left hand of the Madonna, which appears separated from her arm that holds the child, or the right foot, which is incorrectly portrayed in terms of perspective. This might lead us to detect in the artist a lack of sense of body volume and spatial depth, a mastery of his trade that is still incomplete, and to rate the work ultimately as a typical practice exercise in the style of Donatello (Forcellino). Yet there is another notable aspect, in which consists the special artistic value of the work, revealing Michelangelo's virtuoso compositional skill, namely "the coherence with which the truly plastic events of *Madonna of the Steps* are rendered into a stylization that endures up to the surface" (Benkard).

In April 1492, there was an abrupt interruption to Michelangelo's early creative period: Lorenzo de' Medici, his crucial mentor, died at the age of forty-four. While for Michelangelo the ruler's death meant the loss of his artistic and social base, for the republic of Florence it represented the beginning of a profound and enduring political and religious crisis that shook its very foundations toward the end of the fifteenth century and brought the fall of the powerful Medici. Michelangelo then returned to his father's house.

Madonna of the Steps, ca. 1490–92.
Marble, 22½ x 16 in. (57.1 x 40.5 cm). Casa Buonarroti, Florence.

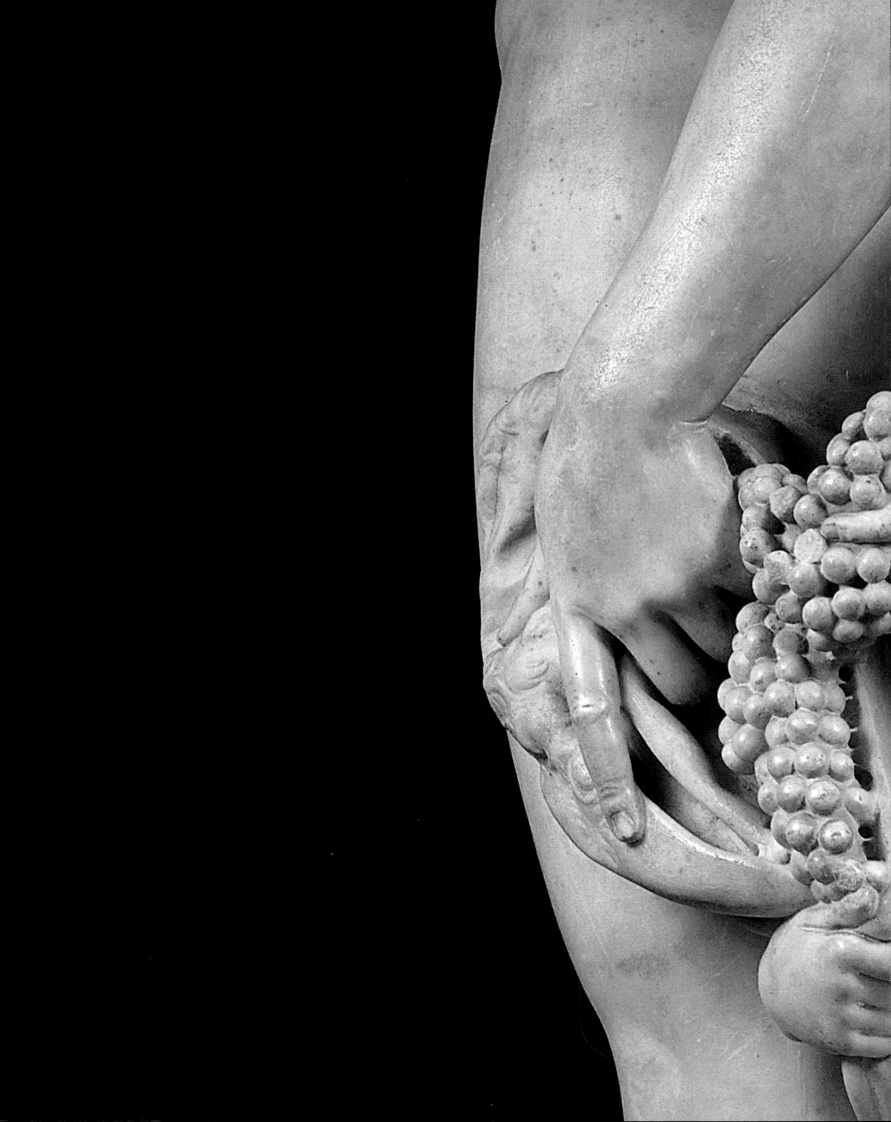

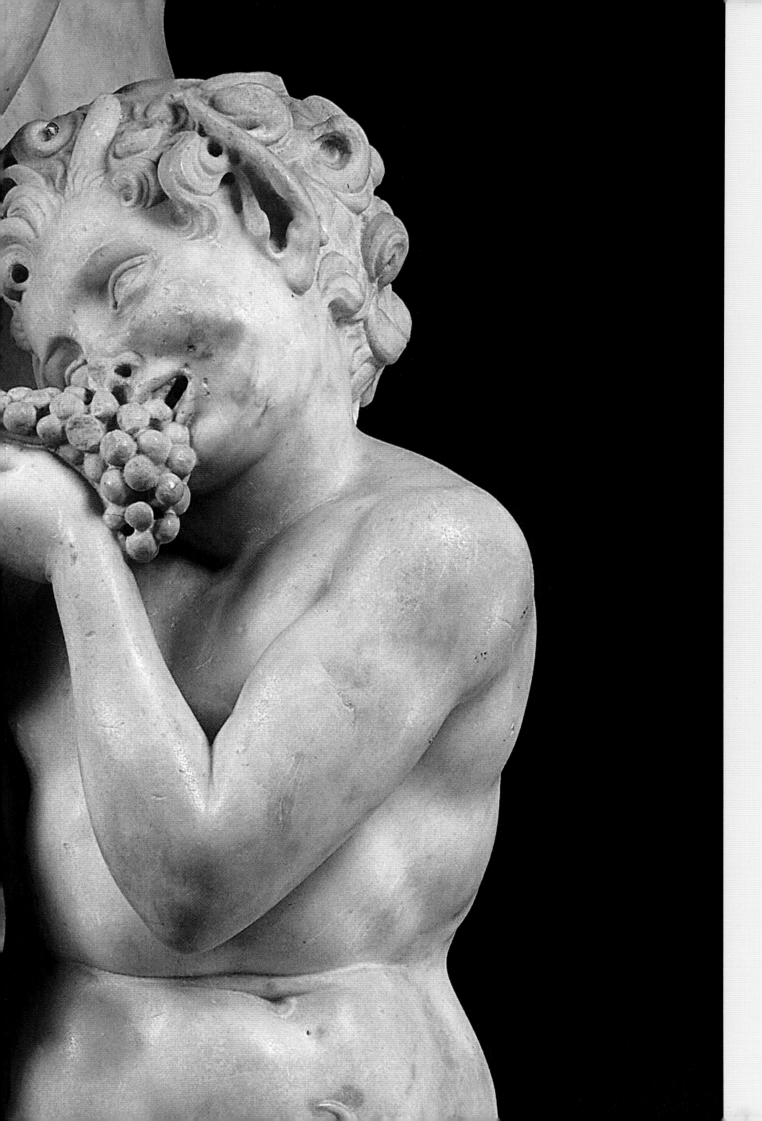

THE END OF THE QUATTROCENTO

Workshop of Agnolo Bronzino, *Portrait of Piero II de' Medici*, ca. 1555–65. Oil on tin, 6 x 4¾ in. (15 x 12 cm). Medici Museum, Florence.

▷ **Giorgio Vasari**, *The People Paying Tribute to Lorenzo de' Medici*, ca. 1555. Pen, watercolor, pencil, and white lead on blue paper, 13¼ x 10¼ in. (33.8 x 25.8 cm). Gabinetto dei Disegni e delle Stampe degli Uffizi, Florence.

PAGES 22–3
Drunken Bacchus (detail of the satyr), 1496–97. Marble. Bargello Museum, Florence.

"Has such a Bacchus ever been seen?" asked Karl Frey. The famous Michelangelo scholar, who understood the "painterly modeling" of the *Bacchus* as an expression of Michelangelo's study of antique models, also regarded the stronger emphasis on the structure of the body as evidence of the young genius's neutrality toward the colossal figures of antiquity.

MICHELANGELO'S FLIGHT FROM FLORENCE

Lorenzo de' Medici "the Magnificent" died the night of April 8, 1492. His death shook Florence, which lost in him not only a leading political figure but also a ruler whose actions had generally been deeply imbued with the spirit of the Renaissance. His sudden demise inspired famous contemporaries such as Pope Innocent VIII, as he too approached death, to gloomy premonitions that peace throughout Italy was now in danger. He was to be proven right.

The closing decade of the fifteenth century was characterized by smoldering struggles for supremacy in Europe between Habsburg Spain and France. King Charles VIII of France staked a claim to the kingdom of Naples and in his course through Italy in fall 1494 stood before the gates of Florence. The king threatened to sack the city if he was not granted free passage. Both the city and Piero II de' Medici (1472–1503, ill. p.24), who was just twenty years old and had taken over the principality from his father Lorenzo, were totally unprepared for this threat. Piero de' Medici proved to be an immature, careless, and, above all, politically imprudent ruler, whose failure finally led to the expulsion of the Medici from Florence in November 1494.

It can no longer be stated for certain how Michelangelo's relationship with the young Piero de' Medici developed. The more recent Michelangelo literature tends to suppose that a close friendship existed between them until the artist's flight from Florence in October 1494. According to Condivi and Vasari, Piero held Michelangelo in high regard, having, Vasari reports, often sent for him "when he wanted to buy antiques such as cameos and other engraved stones." There are alternative views, however, that Michelangelo never managed to reconcile himself to Piero's vanity and suffered from the loss of his patron Lorenzo de' Medici. Moreover, in fall 1494 came the deaths of Angelo Poliziano and Giovanni Pico della Mirandola, who belonged to the circle of outstanding scholars that Lorenzo had gathered at his court.

During this period, Michelangelo began his studies in anatomy. Although the dissection of corpses was strictly forbidden—on pain of being burned as a heretic—the prior of

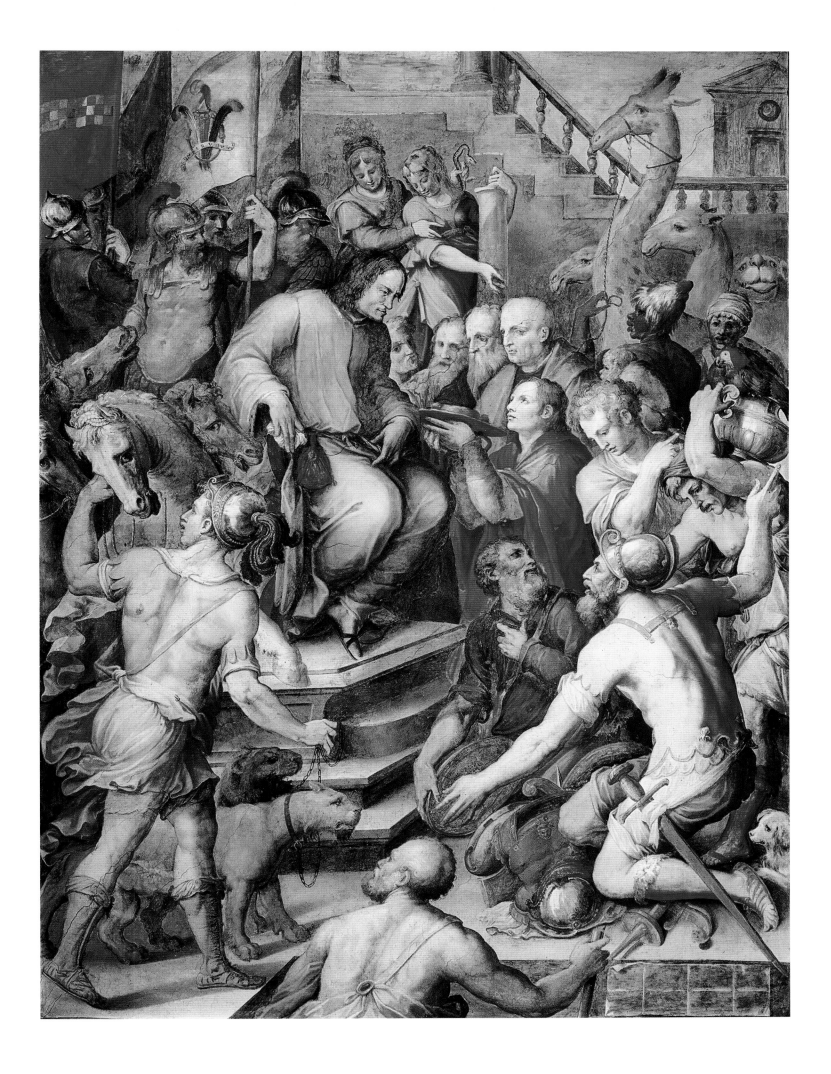

only did Florence then forfeit its major fortresses, the cities of Pisa and Livorno also fell to the French king. With this act, Piero turned the people against him. On his return, the city was hostile to him, which led to a popular uprising that resulted in the fall of the Medici. On November 9, 1494, Piero had to flee with his brothers Giuliano and Giovanni, who later became Pope Leo X. The Medici Palace was plundered, as well as the famous garden with antique statues in which Michelangelo had once studied. Many of the valuable art treasures that Lorenzo had assembled in his palace were auctioned in 1495 in Orsanmichele, tearing apart one of the most important art collections of the fifteenth century.

In the following period, a Florentine republic was established under the intellectual leadership of the Dominican monk and repentance-preacher Girolamo Savonarola. In the time of Lorenzo the Magnificent, Savonarola had already derided Florence as a moral cesspit and railed against the rule of the Medici in his impassioned sermons. Michelangelo himself is thought to have belonged to his vast audience, numbering 12,000 to 14,000, according to the Florentine historiographer Luca Landucci. Savonarola was seeking a fundamental reform of Florentine society; he not only condemned Neoplatonic teachings but also disapproved of every form of secular art.

Attributed to Michelangelo, *Crucifix*, ca. 1492–93.
Polychrome painted wood, 54¾ x 53¼ in. (139 x 135 cm).
Santo Spirito, Florence.

"And they say that he [Savonarola] is a rank heretic, and that is why he may under all circumstances come to Rome, to prophesy a bit here; and then he will be canonized, which would satisfy all his followers."

Michelangelo in a letter of March 10, 1498, to his brother Buonarroto in Florence.

the Augustine monastery Santo Spirito provided him with a room as well as some corpses so that he could carry out his anatomical studies in secret. However, Michelangelo had to abandon these because according to Condivi "his long handling of them had so affected his stomach that he could neither eat nor drink salutarily." In a gesture of goodwill, Michelangelo is thought to have given the prior a slightly less than life-size wooden crucifix (ill. p.26). This crucifix, which is said to have been placed over the high altar of the monastery church, was later mislaid and only reappeared in 1964. To this day, its attribution to Michelangelo is disputed.

Events in Florence then took a definite turn for the worse. Piero de' Medici squandered his father's entire legacy of achievements: the balance of power that characterized the relations between the individual states in Italy, the *Italia bilanciata*, Florence's own position of dominance, and the peace established in Tuscany. When King Charles VIII of France stood with his troops before Florence (ill. p.12), Piero was totally overwhelmed by the situation. He soon abandoned his initial opposition; he set himself above the Signoria and negotiated high-handedly with the king himself. On October 26, 1494, he rode toward Charles VIII and surrendered without a fight. Not

Thus in Florence, books, pictures, and other works of art were piled onto burning pyres and destroyed. Yet even by May 1498, Savonarola's own pyres were blazing. He had defied the decrees of the power-obsessed Borgia Pope Alexander VI (ill. p.38), who had excommunicated him and banned him from preaching. Piero de' Medici made several vain attempts to reestablish his rule over the city following Savonarola's death and the resurgence of the Medici partisans. In 1503, when he was less than thirty years old, he drowned in the Garigliano River during the battles between the French and the Spanish for Naples.

Michelangelo had already recognized the danger posed to him by the fall of the Medici and had fled Florence around October 10, 1494. He traveled first to Venice, but his stay there

Giovanni Bellini, *Sacred Conversation*, ca. 1490–1500.
Tempera on wood, 29½ x 33 in. (75 x 84 cm).
Galleria dell'Accademia, Venice.

was unsuccessful because he was unable to find a patron. Venetian painting at that time was under the influence of the brothers Gentile and Giovanni Bellini (ill. p.27); the latter was tutoring Titian. Michelangelo's stay in Venice lasted only one month. He then traveled to Bologna, where he made the momentous acquaintance of Gianfrancesco Aldovrandi, a Bolognese nobleman. Aldovrandi extricated Michelangelo from an awkward situation—at the behest of Giovanni II Bentivoglio, who ruled over Bologna at that time, every stranger who entered the city had to receive a seal. Michelangelo omitted to do this, and was consequently ordered to pay a fine of fifty Bolognese lire. Since he did not have the means to pay it, he was imprisoned. Aldovrandi, who had heard of the incident, arranged for Michelangelo to be released and took him in as a guest at his house. Michelangelo stayed there for one year.

Aldovrandi found Michelangelo his only commission during this stay in Bologna, which was to complete the figure ornamentation for St. Dominic's tomb in San Domenico that had been left unfinished by the Bolognese sculptor Niccolò

dell'Arca (ca. 1435–94). Michelangelo created in total three sculptures during 1494–95 for this sarcophagus, known as *Arca di S. Domenico*: a kneeling, candelabrum-bearing angel (ill. p.31), and statues of *St. Petronius* (ill. p.28) and *St. Proculus* (ill. p.29). Vasari and Condivi mention only the angel and the Petronius figure, for which Michelangelo received 30 ducats from Aldovrandi. The fact that he was allowed little maneuvering room in the composition of the figure ornamentation by dell'Arca's instructions is attested by the direct comparison of the candelabrum-bearing angels of the two artists—stylistically there is no difference to be observed here; they appear as companion pieces made by the same hand (ill. pp.30, 31). In the *St. Proculus* sculpture, however, the young Michelangelo's creative powers are impressively revealed. The statue represents the soldier Proculus, one of the patron saints of Bologna, who died a martyr in AD 303. Michelangelo represented him with a flag laid over his left shoulder, which is the traditional attribute of a saint. The statue, which suffered extensive damage in the sixteenth century and was only poorly

Tomb of St. Dominic, 1265–67, begun by Nicola Pisano, crowning by Niccolò dell'Arca 1469–73. Marble.
Basilica of San Domenico, Bologna.

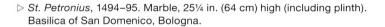

▷ *St. Petronius*, 1494–95. Marble, 25¼ in. (64 cm) high (including plinth).
Basilica of San Domenico, Bologna.

restored, is infused with a keen anticipation of movement. The viewer senses that a moment of action is directly approaching: Is the clenched fist about to open? The resolute gaze of Proculus, the tension between the standing leg and the free leg, and the slight turn of the hips all reinforce this impression. The tension and the restrained energy that may erupt at any moment already prefigures the famous *David* (ill. p.43).

In winter 1495, Michelangelo again returned to his father in Florence. At that time, the Dominican monk and repentance-preacher Savonarola had succeeded in implementing a new republican constitution. The former rulers of the House of Medici had been driven out, but the descendants of another line of the family remained in the city: these were Lorenzo and Giovanni, the cousins of the deceased Lorenzo the Magnificent and the sons of Lorenzo's uncle, Pierfrancesco de' Medici. They had supported the expulsion of the hapless Piero and

now occupied influential positions in the new government. Michelangelo soon befriended Lorenzo di Pierfrancesco, one of Pierfrancesco de' Medici's two sons. For him he created the figure of a small *St. John*, as well as a sleeping *Cupid*, neither of which has been preserved. A legend has grown up around *Cupid*, which ultimately had a happy outcome for Michelangelo.

Vasari and Condivi report that it was Lorenzo di Pierfrancesco's idea to sell *Cupid* to Rome as an antique original. Declared as such, the figure is supposed to finally have entered the possession of Cardinal Raffaele Riario in Rome through an intermediary in return for 200 ducats. The intermediary, however, deceived not only the cardinal but also Michelangelo

St. Proculus, 1494–95. Marble, 23 in. (58.5 cm) high (including plinth).
Basilica of San Domenico, Bologna.

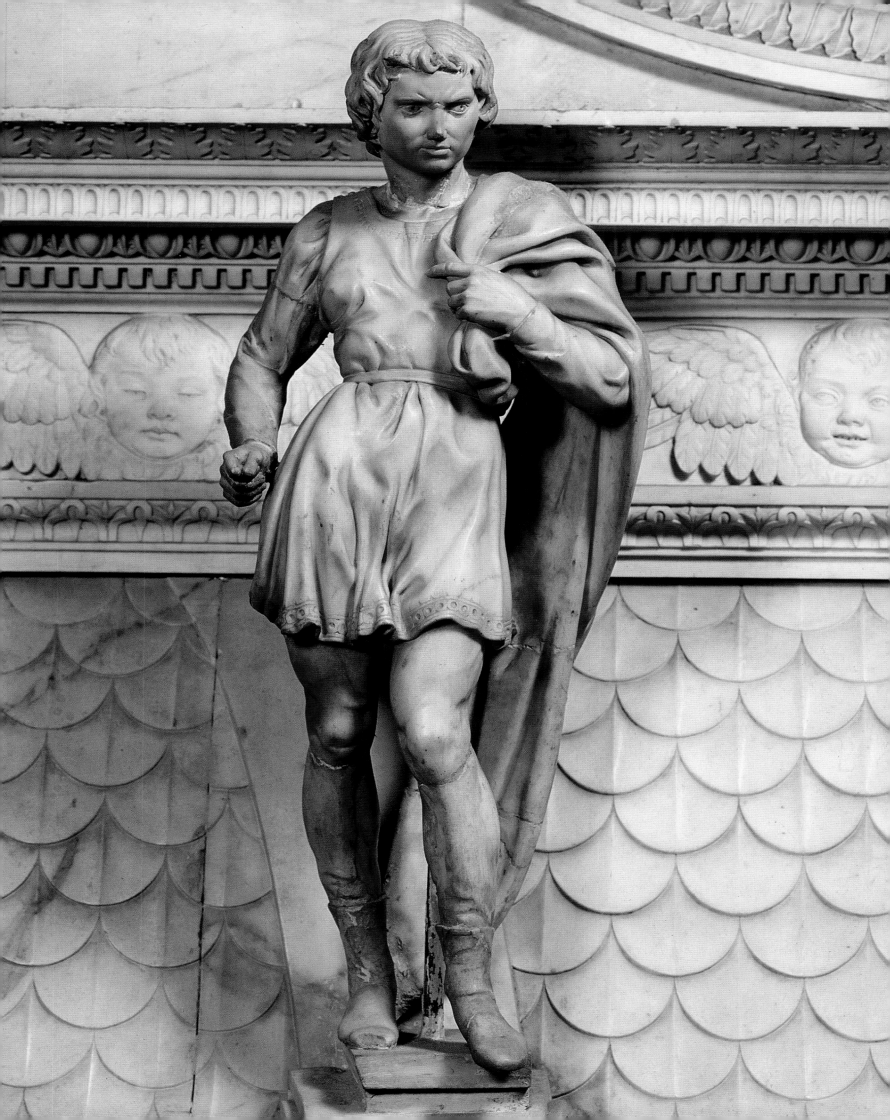

by paying him only 30 ducats. The deception was uncovered and the cardinal found out how the figure had originated; he demanded his money back, which he received. Nevertheless, the cardinal was prepared to become reconciled with Michelangelo, who had himself been deceived, and he invited him to Rome. Thus, in summer 1496 at the age of twenty-one years, the artist embarked on his first visit to the Eternal City. In the next four decades, his life was to unfold between his native city of Florence and Rome.

Cardinal Raffaele was a great-nephew of Pope Sixtus IV (1471–84) and an opponent of the Medici, who had played a decisive role in the Pazzi conspiracy of 1478 in which Giuliano de' Medici had been murdered. Raffaele had built up an outstanding collection of antique sculptures in Rome. As Michelangelo reported in a letter of July 2, 1496, to Lorenzo di Pierfrancesco de' Medici, the cardinal asked him whether he would dare to produce "something beautiful" like the antiquities in his collection. Michelangelo replied, "that I could not do anything as fine, but that he should see what I could do. We have bought a piece of marble for a life-sized figure and on Monday [July 4] I shall begin work." From this "piece of marble" Michelangelo went to work on *Drunken Bacchus*, which

Melozzo da Forti, *Pope Sixtus IV Appoints Platina Prefect of the Library*, 1477. Fresco. Vatican, Pinocoteca, Room IV, Rome.

> *"This splendid achievement showed that Michelangelo could surpass every other sculptor of the modern age."*
>
> *Vasari on Michelangelo's Bacchus.*

won him great acclaim from contemporaries and also marked the transition to his artistic maturity (ill. p.32).

This sculpture was the first life-size marble statue of an antique god made in Christian times. With it, Michelangelo was competing with the ancients, but at the same time he made some innovations that earned the work a unique position in anticipating the sculpture of the sixteenth century. This is mainly due to the emancipation from classical *contrapposto*, and yet can be also recognized from a swaying motion in the posture of the wine god. Everything seems calculated to reproduce

Drunken Bacchus, 1496–97. Marble, 80 in. (203 cm) high (including plinth). Bargello Museum, Florence.

PAGE 30
Niccolò dell'Arca, *Angel Candelabrum*, ca. 1470–73. Marble, 20½ in. (52 cm) high (including plinth). Basilica of San Domenico, Bologna.

PAGE 31
Kneeling Angel (Angel Candelabrum), 1494–95. Marble, 20¼ in. (51.5 cm) high (including plinth). Basilica of San Domenico, Bologna.

this movement: while the head of Bacchus is inclined slightly forward, the upper body is turning very slightly backward, and the stomach protrudes in a curve. In a slightly bent posture, the wine god stands there, his face wreathed with vine branches, a faint smile on his lips, which also indicates drunkenness. In his right hand, Bacchus is holding a drinking bowl, in his left a tiger's skin; he is accompanied by a small satyr who is chewing on a grapevine. The group is arranged for total visibility, and the multiplicity of possible viewpoints allows for its installation in an antiquities garden. Masterly and to that extent ahead of their time are the gentle composition of the muscles, as well as the supple rounding of the limbs and joints. Both this and the androgynous quality of the Bacchus figure were emphasized by Vasari.

Opinions concerning the symbolic content of the work differ to this day. In Condivi's view, the main import of the expressive content is the moral message that "he who lets himself be lured to that extent by the senses and by the craving for that fruit and its liquor ends by giving up his life to it." Yet it seems superficial to assume that Michelangelo connected the antique theme solely with this moral warning. Consideration must instead be given here to the influence of Neoplatonic philosophy, which Michelangelo encountered at Lorenzo's court primarily through the influence of Marsilio Ficino (1433–99). Referring back to Plato's *Phaedo*, in which Socrates attributes to Dionysus the divine state of initiation, Ficino indicated in his work of 1469, *De amore* (in which he reflects on Plato's *Symposium on Love*), four kinds of divine rapture that lift the human soul to the higher realms. Mystical rapture he thus attributed to Dionysus, the Greek counterpart to the Roman Bacchus, as that state that brings the soul into consonance and unifies it with a whole, allowing the glimpse of divine beauty.

Bacchus is moreover an example of Michelangelo's deliberate "correction" of facts in his biography. Thus, he did not balk at denying that Cardinal Riario was his patron and claiming that he had received not a single commission from him during his first year in Rome, so that both Vasari and Condivi name the Roman nobleman Jacopo Galli as the patron for *Bacchus*. The cardinal's payments to the artist are, however, conclusively verified. This reveals a certain unscrupulousness on the artist's part, given that it was those same payments from Riario that enabled Michelangelo at that time to send adequate support to his family, who were in dire financial straits.

Enguerrand Quarton, *Pietà of Villeneuve-les-Avignon*, ca. 1455.
Oil on canvas, 64¼ x 85¾ in. (163 x 218 cm). Musée du Louvre, Paris.

THE ARTISTIC BREAKTHROUGH

The work on the *Bacchus* sculpture occupied Michelangelo for one year, and it was completed in 1497. Afterward he turned briefly to painting and created the so-called *Manchester Madonna*, a tempera painting on a wooden panel that has remained unfinished (ill. p.34). The painting is now in London's National Gallery and, along with the similarly unfinished oil painting of an *Entombment* dating from this period, belongs to the works attributed to Michelangelo by research since the 1990s; both are "*intermezzi* in painting," for Michelangelo's creative activity around the turn of the century is far outshone by his sculptural works.

The theme of the Virgin Mary with her dead son was to be realized in a work that sealed Michelangelo's fame when he was just twenty-four years old and indisputably signified his conclusive artistic breakthrough. On August 27, 1498, Michelangelo agreed to a contract with the French bishop Jean Bilhères de Lagraulas, cardinal of Saint-Denis, to produce a marble Pietà for which he was to receive 455 gold ducats. The contract from the bishop, who was King Charles VIII's envoy in the Vatican, was given to Michelangelo by the Roman banker Jacopo Galli.

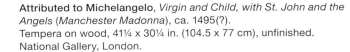

Attributed to Michelangelo, *Virgin and Child, with St. John and the Angels (Manchester Madonna)*, ca. 1495(?).
Tempera on wood, 41¼ x 30¼ in. (104.5 x 77 cm), unfinished.
National Gallery, London.

The original installation site for *Pietà* (ill. pp.35, 36, 39) was St. Petronilla's Chapel in the old St. Peter's, the chapel of the French kings, which was demolished before 1520 to make way for the new building of St. Peter's. *Pietà* has been on view only since 1794 in its current position in the first side chapel (Cappella della Pietà) in the right side aisle of St. Peter's.

Michelangelo represents in *Pietà* the iconographic type of Our Lady of Sorrows that was widespread in the fourteenth and fifteenth centuries, especially in France and Germany (ill. p.34). The Virgin Mary is seated slightly raised on a cliff; hidden in her lap rests the dead Christ, who has been taken

Pietà, 1498–99.
Marble, 68½ in. (174 cm) high (including plinth).
Vatican, St. Peter's, Rome.

In breaking away from tradition, Michelangelo shaped the theme of the lamentation of Christ by showing the Virgin Mary, not grief-stricken in the full force of her despairing suffering, but in her quiet pain and her devotion to fate. The masterly treatment of the marble was described by Robert Coughlan as follows: "No other sculpture by him surpasses it in perfection. Its surface is so smooth that it shimmers, the gentle modeling gives the marble the effect of flesh and blood, and the rich arrangement of folds in the garments gives the whole work a vibrant energy" (Coughlan).

The highly elaborate plastic development is shown in the coat of Mary's garments; in a polished cascade of small folds that lead down to the hem, they flow around the gentle figure of Mary.

down from the Cross, bearing the stigmata of the Crucifixion on his hands, feet, and chest. The body of the life-size Christ figure appears tilted to one side, and the head of Christ is sunk lifelessly backward. With her right arm, the Virgin is holding her son's upper body under the armpit to prevent the dead body from sliding off her lap. Support is given by her right leg, which is raised by the stratagem of the stone block placed under her right foot; an equilibrium is achieved here between support and burden. The gracefulness and the beauty of the figures are striking.

In the literature, Christ's facial features have repeatedly been compared with those of a young Apollo. The tenderness of the Virgin Mary's countenance betrays none of her inner torment and grief; she appears deep in contemplative devotion (ill. pp.35, 39). Her restrained grief is reinforced by the gesture of her left hand. Here the dialog with the viewer becomes completely evident: the open upturned palm evokes a questioning gesture; she seems to the viewer to be presenting the dead Christ with a questioning "Why?" Mary's face and Christ's body are extremely finely and gently sculpted, and the curves of Christ's body are remarkably smooth. In contrast to this stands the abundance of material and plasticity of the arrangement of folds in Mary's robes.

The striking youthfulness of the Virgin Mary, whose countenance hardly indicates any difference in age from her son, stirred violent criticism among contemporaries. In her youthfulness, the mother resembles an iconographic transposition of the first few lines from St. Bernard's famous prayer in the thirty-third canto of "Paradise" in *The Divine Comedy*: "O Virgin, Mother, daughter of your son" (Dante).

More recent Michelangelo research has devoted attention to a detail in the group of figures that was previously given little consideration. This is the tree stump that gives support to the left foot of the dead Christ, which can almost be missed. Kerstin Schwedes sees this as an "ominous symbolic motif" and a "clear warning to the viewer to think in humble contrition of the Son of God made man who, in contrast to human beings with their worldly preoccupations, lived without sin and through whose earthly death human beings can enjoy the grace of eternal

life, which of course at the same time calls the worshiper to repentance" (Schwedes).

Later on, in the fresco of *The Fall* in the Sistine Chapel, Michelangelo took up this iconographic motif again. The unparalleled effect of *Pietà* and the "new and independent interpretation of the sculptural representations of the *Pietà*" (ibid.) revealed here are based on that same intensive dialog between the viewer and the work. This is a dialog characterized primarily by the emotional impact made on the viewer by the expressive and gestural language of the figures, which also challenges the viewer to engage with the theme of life and death and, not least, to recognize the immanent symbolic content of the work.

The easily legible signature chiseled in Latin roman-type block capitals on the belt of the coat over the upper body of the Virgin Mary—"MICHAEL.A(N)GELUS.BONARTUS.

> "When I was discussing this one day with Michelangelo, he answered, 'Don't you know that women who are chaste remain much fresher than those who are not?... Indeed, I will go further and say that this freshness and flowering of youth, apart from being preserved by her in this natural way, may also conceivably have been given divine assistance in order to prove to the world the virginity and perpetual purity of the mother.'"
>
> *Michelangelo according to Condivi.*

Pietà (detail of the hand of Christ), 1498–99.
Marble.
Vatican, St. Peter's, Rome.

The immense popularity that Michelangelo gained through the work is illustrated by Vasari's praise: "It would be impossible for any craftsman or sculptor, no matter how brilliant, ever to surpass the grace or design of this work or try to cut and polish the marble with the skill that Michelangelo displayed. For the *Pietà* was a revelation of all the potentialities and force of the art of sculpture...." (Vasari).

FLORENT.FACIEBAT" (Michelangelo Buonarroti of Florence made this)—remained the first and only signature that Michelangelo ever added to one of his works.

According to Vasari, Michelangelo inscribed this signature because he was annoyed that there seemed to be some debate about the sculpture's authorship. One day some visitors from Lombardy are supposed to have gathered in front of the sculpture. When they asked who made it, they were told that this had been a certain "Gobbo from Milan." Michelangelo, who supposedly overheard this, is said as a result to have shut himself in St. Peter's during the night with a lamp and a chisel and chiseled his name into the Madonna's belt. Whether the episode actually took place in that way is open to doubt. It is,

Spanish School, *Portrait of Pope Alexander VI*, fifteenth century.
Oil on canvas.
Vatican, Pinacoteca, Rome.

however, illuminating because it gives rise to one of the most plausible explanations for Michelangelo's signature among the multiplicity of interpretations that have occurred to this day. Actually the above-mentioned "Gobbo" is a word that means the hunchback in Italian. The soubriquet was in fact commonly applied to a sculptor from Milan named Cristoforo Solari (ca. 1460–1527), who enjoyed the highest regard in Rome with Pope Alexander VI (ill. p.38). Against this background, it appears conceivable that Michelangelo was intentionally giving expression to his Florentine origins, possibly identifying himself as a man from Tuscany who was challenging the Lombardian's "dominion."

Michelangelo completed *Pietà* in 1499. His patron, the cardinal of Saint-Denis, died in August 1499 without having had sight of the completed work. It became Michelangelo's first masterpiece, which spread his fame as a sculptor far and wide, bringing him at the beginning of 1501 to the notice of another cardinal, Francesco Piccolomini, who later became Pope Pius III (1503).

Cardinal Piccolomini suggested that Michelangelo complete the figure ornamentation on the Piccolomini altar in Siena Cathedral. The altar had been created by the Lombardian sculptor Andrea di Cristoforo Bregno, who had done extensive work in Rome in the late fifteenth century and had completed the reredos of the Piccolomini altar in 1503.

The intermediary for the cardinal's commissioning of Michelangelo was the highly esteemed Piero Soderini, who in 1502 was elected for life to the office of the highest administrative officials of Florence, the Gonfalionere della Giustizia, and steered the fate of the republic of Florence. The city was just emerging from the dark events of the final years of the fifteenth century and the profound repercussions following the expulsion of the Medici. After Savonarola's execution on May 23, 1498, on the Piazza della Signoria, a government had been installed that consisted principally of representatives of that section of the bourgeoisie to which the Buonarroti were also close.

Given the prevailing atmosphere in Rome, it must have seemed to Michelangelo that a return to Florence might be the far better option; conditions in the Eternal City at that time were anything but good. With the unbridled Borgia pope, Alexander VI, who entered the annals of history with scandals such as his incestuous relationship with his daughter Lucrezia, the city degenerated noticeably into immorality, filth, and stench, and the city districts had to in essence rule themselves, since any effective municipal authority was lacking. To this was added the financial difficulties of his family, whom Michelangelo constantly supported with sums of money, as his letters from Rome at this time attest; thus he writes, for example, on August 19, 1497, "However, what you ask of me I'll send you, even if I should have to sell myself as a slave." In fact, Michelangelo returned to Florence in early 1501.

On June 5, he signed a contract for fifteen niche figures for the Piccolomini altar in Siena Cathedral, for which he could anticipate an excellent fee of 500 ducats. Yet what was to prove a more decisive consequence for him was another commission that he received in August 1501 from the republic of Florence: the colossal statue of *David*, to which Michelangelo himself constantly referred as *"il Gigante,"* that was to become a symbol of the new-won freedom of the Florentine republic.

Pietà (detail of the upper body of Mary), 1498–99.
Marble. Vatican, St. Peter's, Rome.

III. EARLY CREATIVE YEARS IN FLORENCE

EARLY CREATIVE YEARS IN FLORENCE

Donatello, *David with the Head of Goliath*, ca. 1440.
Bronze, 62¼ in. (158 cm) high. Bargello Museum, Florence.

PAGES 40–41
The Holy Family with St. John the Baptist (Doni Tondo)
(detail from Mary's garments), 1503–04.
Tempera on wood. Uffizi Gallery, Florence.

PAGES 44–5
David (details), 1501–04.
Galleria dell'Accademia, Florence.

"IL GIGANTE": *DAVID*—A COMMISSION FROM THE REPUBLIC

The members of the Duomo site office had entrusted the Florentine sculptor Agostino di Duccio (1418–after 1481) with the commission of a monumental figure as early as 1464. Yet, like the sculptor Antonio Rossellino (1427–79), who followed him, Duccio failed at the project; they left the vast block of marble intended for this, which came from a quarry above Carrara, in a rough-hewn state. However, the Cathedral Office of Works and the Florentine wool-weavers' guild wanted the statue completed, and so on August 16, 1501, Michelangelo, just twenty-six years old, received from the Florence Cathedral Office of Works the commission for *David*, which was to occupy him until April 1504. As Vasari reports, Michelangelo began the work by erecting a scaffold of boards around the block that was only dismantled when the completed statue was moved to its installation site on the Piazza della Signoria in May 1504.

The story of the biblical hero David, who goes bravely into battle against the enemy army of the Philistines and defeats the giant Goliath with his catapult, is known from the Book of Samuel (1 Samuel 17). In Florentine sculpture, artists had already transposed the theme many times before Michelangelo. Some famous examples that preceded Michelangelo's *David* are the bronze statues of Donatello (ill. p.42) and Andrea del Verrocchio (ill. p.46). However, unlike his predecessors, Michelangelo does not represent David as a triumphant victor who has defeated the adversary, with his sword in his hand and Goliath's head at his feet like a macabre trophy; his *David* is inspired with another message.

Michelangelo presents us with his larger than life-size hero by making recourse to the classical *contrapposto* in which the body's weight rests on one leg (ill. p.43). The figure is infused with an inner anticipation in its concentration on the next moment of action. The fiercely resolute gaze, the raised

▷ *David*, 1501–04. Marble, 203¼ in. (516 cm) high (including plinth).
Galleria dell'Accademia, Florence.

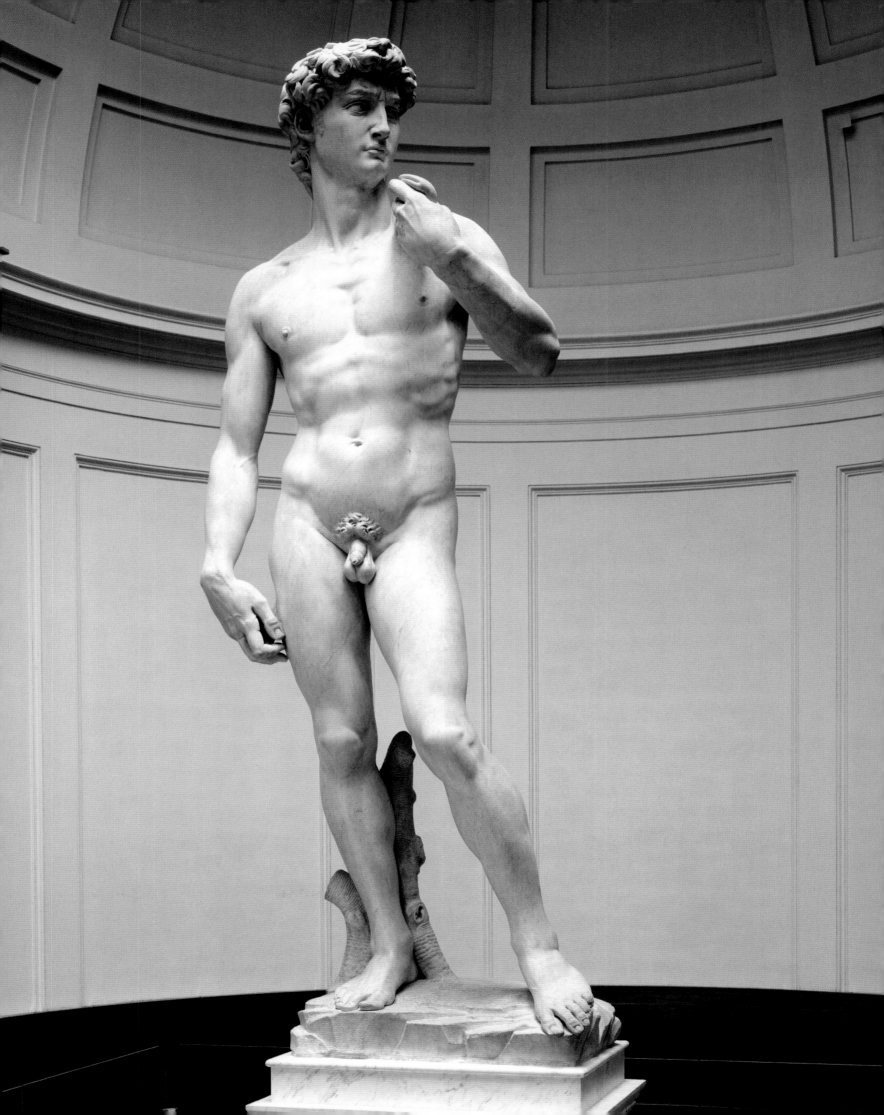

Andrea del Verrocchio, *David*, ca. 1472–76.
Bronze, 49¼ in. (125 cm) high. Bargello Museum, Florence.

▷ Study for *David* (?), 1503–04.
Pen, 14¾ x 7¾ in. (37.5 x 19.5 cm). Musée du Louvre, Paris.

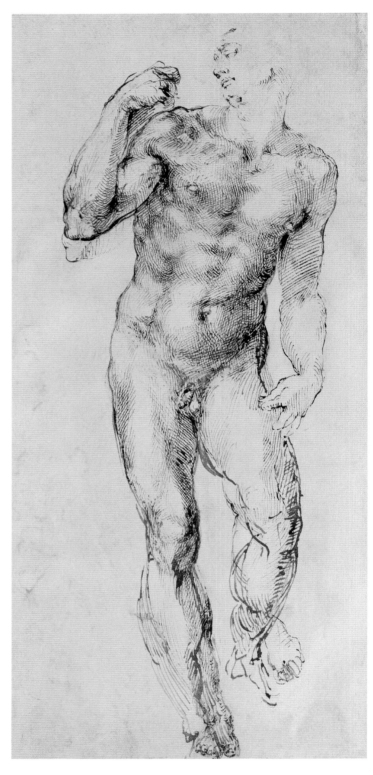

eyebrows, the wrinkled forehead, and the hugely powerful-looking right hand filled with yearning in which David holds the stone, while his left hand clasps the catapult that is lying over his left shoulder, all bear witness to this. Everything is predicated on the next moment in which David will use the catapult to strike the fatal blow against the enemy.

As Michelangelo presents us with the youthful duelist at the moment of greatest concentration before the actual attack, the artist breaks away from the Florentine tradition and embarks on a radical new path in the composition of the subject. At the same time, a further compositional element in Michelangelo's

▷ *David* (detail of the back and buttocks), 1501–04.
Marble. Galleria dell'Accademia, Florence.

Vasari's praise speaks for itself: "And without any doubt this figure has put in the shade every other statue, ancient or modern, Greek or Roman…such were the satisfying proportions and beauty of the finished work. The legs are skillfully outlined, the slender flanks are beautifully shaped…. The grace of this figure and the serenity of its pose have never been surpassed, nor have the feet, the hands, and the head, whose harmonious proportions and loveliness are in keeping with the rest. To be sure, anyone who has seen Michelangelo's *David* has no need to see anything else by any other sculptor, living or dead" (Vasari).

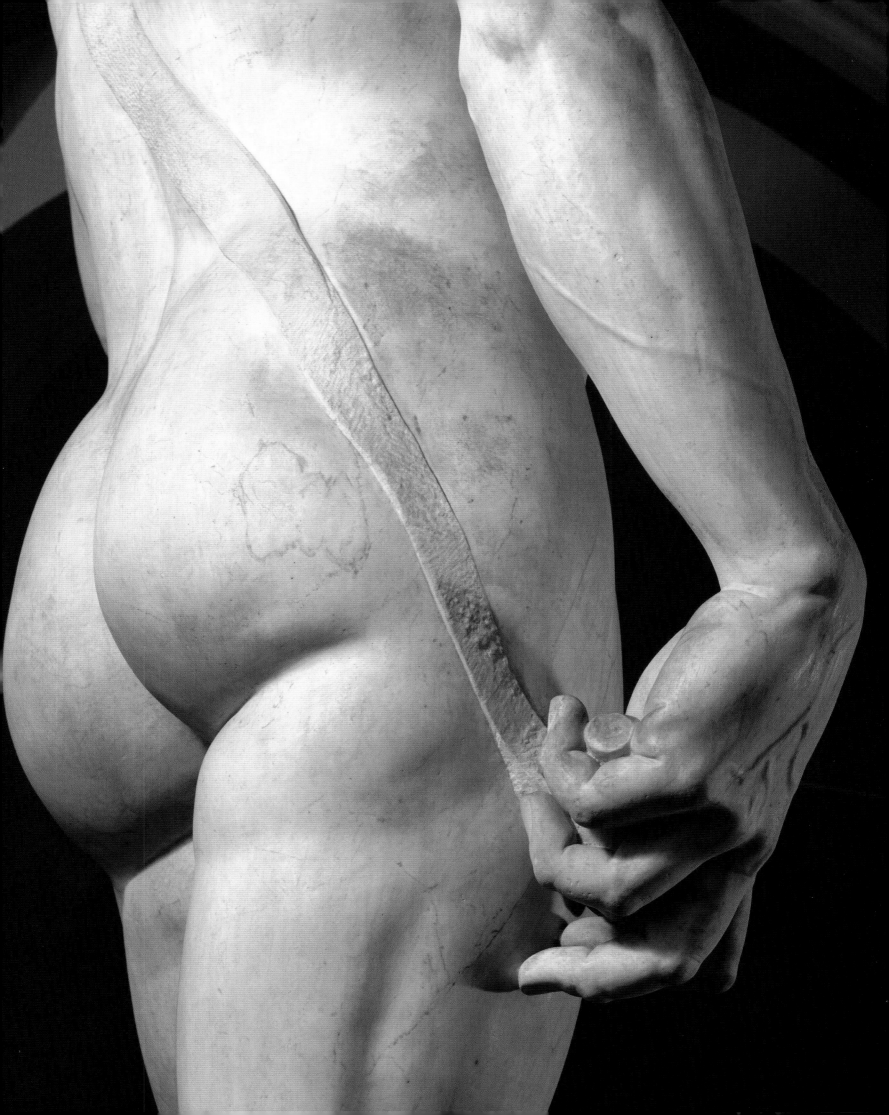

creative work emerges in relation to the representation of the human body: that extreme bodily and mental tension in which he shows us his hero is simultaneously a pause; the viewer senses that this moment is embedded in a temporal sequence— it is that "pregnant moment" that Gotthold Ephraim Lessing described in the eighteenth century in his famous art historical work, *Laocoön: An Essay on the Limits of Painting and Poetry*, with reference to the *Laocoön Group* (ill. p.48), supposedly originating from the first century before Christ. In contrast to Vergil's account, in which Laocoön screams, flouting the law of beauty in Lessing's view, the Greek sculpture shows him only sighing. This is precisely what Lessing saw as that "pregnant moment" of the most acute tension that inspires the viewer's imagination to understand something beyond what he has seen.

David received great recognition from contemporaries as, for example, Raphael attests in the study of *David* (ill. p.48) that he made during his first stay in Florence (Lessing).

On September 8, 1504, *David* was finally unveiled and shown to the citizens of Florence. Michelangelo received 400 scudi (the scudo d'oro, the gold scudo, corresponded to a ducat, with a nominal value of around ten gold marks) from Gonfaloniere Piero Soderini for the work that had occupied him for at least three years. *David* was installed in a symbolically important site: on the Piazza della Signoria, before the entrance to the Palazzo Vecchio. Here it entered the ranks of programmatic sculptures that all symbolize the triumph

Raphael, Study for *David*, back view, 1504–08.
Pen and brown Indian ink, black chalk, 15½ x 8½ in. (39.3 x 21.9 cm).
British Museum, London.

◁ *Laocoön Group*, copy of a Greek bronze, ca. 50 BC.
Marble, 72½ in. (184 cm) high.
Vatican, Cortile del Belvedere, Rome.

of the civil virtues of anger and strength over any threats to freedom and justice, including Baccio Bandinelli's *Hercules and Cactus* and Donatello's *Judith and Holofernes* (see figure in Chronology fold-out), which can still be seen in this same location today (ill. p.63). Michelangelo's biblical hero, who radiates an unconquerable and divinely protected strength and resolution that finally enables him to triumph over evil, became a symbol of the freedom and vigor of the Florentine republic.

Leonardo da Vinci, Study for *The Battle of Anghiari* (detail), 1503–04.
Pen and ink, 5¾ x 6 in. (14.5 x 15.2 cm).
Galleria dell'Accademia, Venice.

Aristotele (Bastiano) da Sangallo, *The Battle of Cascina*, copy from
Michelangelo's cartoon, ca. 1542(?).
Grisaille on wood, 30 x 51¼ in. (76.5 x 130 cm).
Earl of Leicester Collection, Holkham Hall, Norfolk, England.

Study for *The Battle of Cascina*, ca. 1504.
Charcoal, 9¼ x 14 in. (23.5 x 35.5 cm).
Gabinetto dei Disegni e delle Stampe degli Uffizi, Florence.

▷ Study of a battle scene for *The Battle of Cascina* (detail), ca. 1504.
Pen and Indian ink, 7 x 10 in. (17.9 x 25.1 cm).
Ashmolean Museum, University of Oxford, England.

After completing *David*, Michelangelo received from his patron Piero Soderini the commission for a wall painting in the Great Hall of the Palazzo Vecchio, a work that brought him into direct competition with his far senior *uomo universale*, Leonardo da Vinci (1452–1519), who had returned to Florence in 1500. The theme of the wall painting commissioned by Soderini was to be important military victories of the Florentine republic. While Leonardo was commissioned to portray the battle of Anghiari (ill. p.49) in which the Florentines triumphed over the Milanese in 1440, Michelangelo was to portray on the opposite wall the battle of Cascina, which ended in the victory of the Florentines over the Pisans in 1346.

From December 1504, Michelangelo prepared a cartoon—a true-to-scale preliminary drawing—that is not preserved. A copy of this cartoon made by Aristotele (Bastiano) da Sangallo, supposedly around 1542, nevertheless conveys a good likeness of Michelangelo's depiction (ill. p.49). It can be seen once again that Michelangelo uses the theme for a masterly portrayal of the naked human body in motion. Vasari has provided a

highly detailed and vivid description of this cartoon, which he writes of as being filled with "naked men who are bathing because of the heat in the River Arno when suddenly upon attack by the enemy the alarm is raised in the camp...soldiers... some hurrying to arm themselves in order to bring help to their comrades, others buckling on their breastplates, many fastening other pieces of armor on their bodies, and countless more dashing into the fray on horseback...some drummers and other naked figures, with their clothes bundled up, hurrying to get to the fighting, and drawn in various unusual attitudes: some upright, some kneeling or leaning forward, or halfway between one position and another, all exhibiting the most difficult foreshortenings."

Unlike Leonardo, Michelangelo decided to depict not the actual thick of the battle but instead the moment before the battle started. In its portrayal of animated bodies, the work is reminiscent of the early *Battle of the Centaurs* (ill. pp.18–19) in which every superfluous narrative attribute is similarly omitted in favor of the concentration on the figures in action. Michelangelo's cartoon drew great attention

from contemporaries and served many artists of the time in their study of drawing and the treatment of the body (ill. pp.50–51).

Both Michelangelo's and Leonardo's cartoons were destroyed and are known only from copies. Similarly, the wall paintings begun by both artists are not preserved; Leonardo had abandoned work on his fresco in May 1506, and Michelangelo also did not complete the fresco he began in November 1506. In the sixteenth century, the scenes of the painting of the Great Hall that had already been painted on the wall were then painted over by Vasari.

While Michelangelo devoted himself once more in *The Battle of Cascina* to his main subject, the representation of the human body in motion, he also returned to the theme of the Virgin Mary with her son in some of his works during this productive creative period in Florence. In contrast to the *Pietà* in Rome, which established his artistic breakthrough, it is no longer the Lady of Sorrows with the dead Christ but the Madonna with the Christ child who stands at the center of the sculptures.

DONI TONDO AND OTHER MADONNAS

Doni Tondo, the only tempera panel painting that was indisputably executed by Michelangelo (ill. pp.52–3), was commissioned from him by the influential Florentine merchant Agnolo Doni on the occasion of his marriage to Maddalena di Giovanni Strozzi in 1504. The picture, which the Italian art historian Roberto Longhi evaluated in his 1914 work on the history of Italian painting as the absolute masterpiece in Michelangelo's painterly creative work, is to this day regarded as enigmatic in research. Among the art historians of the late nineteenth century, including the famous Jacob Burckhardt, the picture met with disapproval; the Michelangelo scholar Carl Justi even described the play of the joint apparatus of the *Doni Madonna* as "a piece of indoor gymnastics" (Justi). The more modern interpretative approaches tend instead to read it as a representation of the evolution from the heathen age—personified by the naked figures worked out in anatomical detail in the background—to the Christian age, represented by the boy John the Baptist in the right middle ground, also

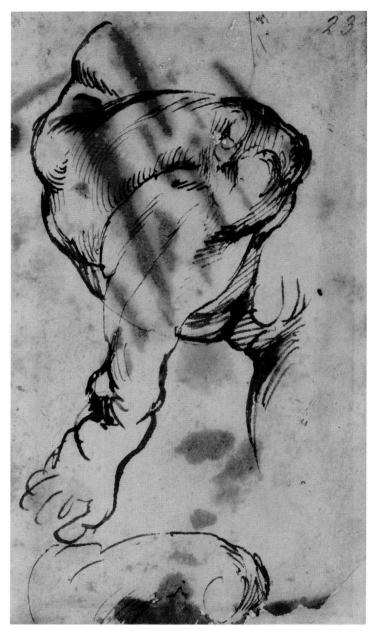

Leg study for *Doni Tondo*, ca. 1503.
Pen and Indian ink, 6 x 3¼ in. (15.3 x 8.2 cm).
Casa Buonarroti, Florence.

a symbol of the Old Testament, and the Holy Family in the foreground, as a symbol of the New Testament.

Striking here is the pronounced dynamism of the composition that creates an immediate illusion of movement in which the central figures are extremely closely interconnected in a unified whole. In the center is the turning movement of the Virgin Mary, who, seated in an unusual pose on the floor and depicted in masterly perspective foreshortening, is lifting

PAGES 52–3
Doni Tondo (detail of *The Holy Family*), 1503–04.
Tempera on wood. Uffizi Gallery, Florence.

up the child. Moreover, the Virgin's muscularly sculpted upper arms give an impression of remarkable energy.

The contours of the figures are sharply defined and the garments are portrayed with extraordinary plasticity, which becomes especially conspicuous in the Madonna's garments (ill. pp.40–41). The coloring is entrancing in its clarity; this picture by Michelangelo was in fact recently restored. It is dominated by the orange–pink–blue triad of the Holy Family group, in which the colors appear metallic, radiating a certain hard and cold quality. This impression is reinforced by the incursion of light, falling clearly and brightly on the garments, the coloring of which is conditioned by the interplay of areas of light and shade. One further detail should be emphasized here: the little boy sitting on the right behind Joseph's left shoulder. According to the more recent interpretations in the Michelangelo literature, this iconographic detail can be understood to have been derived by Michelangelo from the famous *Belvedere Torso* (see figure in Chronology fold-out). This larger than life-size antique marble torso of a seated man by the Athenian sculptor Apollonius, who worked in the first century BC in Rome, is very likely to have been seen by Michelangelo during his initial stay in Rome; according to contemporaries, he is supposed to have referred to himself as "the student of the *Belvedere Torso*."

Doni Tondo is notable not least because it anticipates the figure composition that appeared in the ceiling frescoes of the Sistine Chapel that Michelangelo was to begin in 1508. According to Vasari, the completion of the painting was accompanied by an ignominious squabble between the patron and the artist over the fee: Agnolo Doni, who delivered only 40 ducats to Michelangelo instead of the 70 for which he had asked, sent the artist into such a rage that he finally demanded double the original amount, and Agnolo ultimately paid 140 ducats for it.

Then there are the two Madonna *tondi* that Michelangelo created in these years for the Florentines Bartolomeo Pitti and Taddeo Taddei. Here, also, the patrons' names are attested by Vasari. In both marble reliefs, which have remained unfinished, the tenderness of the Madonna composition is striking in that the Virgin Mary's facial expression in *Pitti Tondo* (ill. p.56) appears very similar to that of *Bruges Madonna* (ill. p.59). Her face is very finely modeled and her gaze is directed into the distance; seated on a block of stone, she holds the Christ child enclosed with her left arm in a firm, protective gesture. The boy leans on the mother, with his right arm resting on a book that she is holding toward him. Behind the Madonna's right shoulder, the head of John the Baptist as a boy is visible. His face is only gently modeled and, in contrast to the plastically worked head of the Christ child, essentially remains in the relief background.

Unlike *Pitti Tondo* with its peaceful radiance, the figures in *Taddei Tondo* present the viewer with a markedly turbulent

The Holy Family with St. John the Baptist (*Doni Tondo*), 1503–04.
Tempera on wood, diameter (including frame) 47¼ in. (120 cm).
Uffizi Gallery, Florence.

"Consider now the Virgin who is pulsing with a supernatural heartbeat… her whole body…accomplishes a light but constant turning movement, it is wonderfully enveloped by the thousandfold chiselled, narrowly folded and smoothly spread robe…. From the Virgin's upper body… emerges a bronze-colored arm, which is revealed with an indescribable plasticity that is emphasized even more strongly by the empty, smooth, hairless armpit." Less effusive, however, is Longhi's description of the naked Christ child, on whose shoulders "has been set a stout, obstinate, unkempt head visibly overburdened with heavy wisps of fluffy hair…." (Longhi).

Madonna and Child with Young John the Baptist
(*Tondo for Bartolomeo Pitti*), ca. 1504–05.
Marble, 33¾ x 32¼ in. (85.5 x 82 cm).
Bargello Museum, Florence.

▷ *Madonna and Child with Young John the Baptist*
(*Tondo for Taddeo Taddei*), ca. 1505.
Marble, diameter 43 in. (109 cm).
Royal Academy of Arts, London.

Leonardo da Vinci, *Virgin and Child with St. Anne*, ca. 1498.
Charcoal, heightened with white, on paper,
55¾ x 41¼ in. (141.5 x 104.6 cm). National Gallery, London.

impression (ill. p.57). The Madonna is portrayed here in profile. Her gaze is directed at the goldfinch—a symbol of the approaching Passion of Christ—that is held by the boy John the Baptist, standing on the left. In the center of the action is the Christ child, who seems to be anxiously seeking refuge in the mother's lap in a violent backward motion. The different lines of movement in the figures are striking: the vertical line of John, the gentle leaning of the Madonna, the horizontal line of the Christ child, who in his movement of flight also becomes a link between the boy John and the mother. The technical virtuosity is attested by the beautifully formed, plastically worked body of the Christ child, as well as the execution of the folds in Mary's garments.

In the different forms of movement that Michelangelo combines in *Taddei Tondo*, more recent research has identified an essential difference from Leonardo da Vinci's Madonna representations, in particular *Virgin and Child with St. Anne* (ill. p.56 and Chronology fold-out). "The way in which the figures diverge in sharp conflict and nevertheless form a unity in all Michelangelo's works remains fundamentally different from Leonardo's Madonna *concetti*, in which the figures emerge harmoniously and seek a place of fulfillment. Michelangelo's art thrives on a wealth of oppositions; Leonardo's mother and child groups thrive on a tenderly felt, highly diverse intimacy with internal concatenations that cannot possibly be dissolved" (Echinger-Maurach).

Through his work on *David*, Michelangelo's fame and standing had spread not only among the families of Florence, but also far beyond the country's borders. Since 1501 he had been working on *Bruges Madonna* (ill. p.59), which he completed around 1504 and sent to the patron, the respected Flemish cloth merchant Jean (Jan) Mouscron in Bruges. The tenderness and grace of the Madonna's countenance, in particular the contemplative facial expression, show strong similarities with the *Pietà* of St. Peter's. Mary's head covering is also very similar to that of *Pietà*. The Christ child reveals a wealth of plasticity; his limbs are beautifully rounded, and he is holding the mother's garments in a playful gesture. In contrast to the traditional Florentine representations, the Christ child is not sitting on the mother's lap but standing upright between her knees. Michelangelo thus introduced an iconographic innovation that was subsequently adopted by his contemporaries, such as Raphael in his famous oil

painting of *Madonna of the Goldfinch*, created in Florence between 1506 and 1507, which can be seen in the Uffizi Gallery today.

The "new image of Christ" revealed in Michelangelo's *Bruges Madonna* is also evaluated by more recent research as a special characteristic of the group. In comparison with the traditional Florentine mother-and-child representations, such as those seen in the works of Donatello or Benedetto da Maiano, "with Michelangelo the child's divinity emerges not through unchildlike gestures or through attributes, but only through its beauty and the freedom in its actions. This is what Lorenzo the Magnificent explains in Ficino's words in the fourth chapter of his work '*De summo bono,' 'il vero ben è dio formoso e bello'* (the true good is God, completed in its rich forms and beautiful), which we find realized in Michelangelo's work" (Echinger-Maurach). This sound analysis again underlines how strongly Michelangelo's education and intellectual molding by the circle of humanists that were currently present at Lorenzo's court are reflected in his creative work.

Further major works from this immensely productive creative period for Michelangelo are four statues for the Piccolomini altar in Siena Cathedral, *St. Peter* and *St. Paul* (ill. pp.60, 61), as well as *St. Pius* and *St. Gregory*—whose creation did not even fulfill one third of the contract signed with Cardinal Francesco Piccolomini in June 1501—and, not least, the apostle figure of *St. Matthew* for Florence Cathedral (ill. p.58).

The unfinished *St. Matthew* is the only preserved apostle figure that proceeded from a major commission that Michelangelo received in April 1503 from the Florentine wool-weavers' guild. The actual scope of the commission provided for the completion of a total of twelve larger than life-size statues of the apostles. The agreement stipulated that, every year, Michelangelo was to complete one of the statues, which were to be installed in Florence Cathedral. In the following period, however, it emerged that Michelangelo could not fulfill this enormous commission because of his other obligations, so the contract was extended for two more years.

On the figure of *St. Matthew*, only the front side of which is worked out from the stone, Michelangelo's *concetto* can very clearly be seen. From the stone, he exposed what was already hidden in it and also transposed it into that energetic quality that is inherent in the figure—in the turning motion, Matthew's body seems almost to push its way out of the stone.

It is still recognizable today how Michelangelo sought to work out the figures from the stone, which can be seen by the chisel markings.

The statue of *St. Matthew* cannot be precisely dated. It seems likely that work on it was interrupted early in 1506, before Michelangelo followed Julius II's summons to Rome in March of that year—he had received 100 ducats for the journey from the pope. Five years after his first visit to Rome, Michelangelo stood, now thirty years old, at the beginning of a new creative chapter, in which he would immortalize his fame.

St. Matthew, ca. 1505–06. Marble, 85¾ in. (218 cm) high, unfinished. Galleria dell'Accademia, Florence.

▷ *Bruges Madonna (Madonna and Child)*, 1501–ca. 1504. Marble, 50½ in. (128 cm) high (including plinth). Notre-Dame, Bruges, Belgium.

PAGE 60
St. Peter, Piccolomini altar, 1501–04.
Marble, 48¾ in. (124 cm) high. Cathedral, Siena.

PAGE 61
St. Paul, Piccolomini altar, 1501–04,
Marble, 50 in. (127 cm) high. Cathedral, Siena.

DAVID AND ITS CONVOLUTED HISTORY

Michelangelo was still working on his colossal statue *David* when, on January 25, 1504, a meeting was held by an expert committee that brought together the most famous Florentine artists, including Leonardo da Vinci, Sandro Botticelli, Antonio da Sangallo, Piero di Cosimo, Lorenzo di Credi, and Filippino Lippi, as well as Michelangelo's childhood friend Francesco Granacci. The committee was to determine the exact installation site of the statue on the Piazza della Signoria and *David* was to underline the political objectives of this central square as a further symbol of the freedom of the republic of Florence.

David in the Galleria dell'Accademia, Florence, with two of the so-called *Boboli Slaves* in the foreground.

After extensive discussion, the committee's decision finally fell on the installation of *David* in front of the Palazzo Vecchio, where it was to replace the statue of Judith beheading Holofernes (see figure in Chronology fold-out). One further proposal, argued for mainly by Giuliano da Sangallo in order to protect the statue from the impact of the climate, was that it should be installed in the roofed Loggia dei Lanzi, which did not receive any support. So in May 1504 the statue was moved from the building yard of Santa Maria del Fiore Cathedral to the piazza. A special scaffold had been built for its transportation, largely in accordance with the plans of Giuliano and Antonio da Sangallo. Four days in total, from May 14 to 18, 1504, were required to travel the approximately 550-yard (500-meter) stretch of road from the cathedral building yard to its arrival at the Piazza della Signoria.

On September 8, 1504, *David* was finally unveiled before the citizens of Florence: a radiant hero, towering high on the plinth, monumental in size, like the ancient gods. However, in the following centuries the statue sustained some damage: just a few years after the installation, a bolt of lightning struck its plinth so hard that the stability was impaired. In 1527, during the uprisings that resulted in the Medici being expelled once again, one of the statue's arms was smashed; during the Counter-Reformation, it was disfigured by the attachment of a sprig to conceal David's sexual organs. In 1813, 1851, and again in 1991, the statue's toes were broken off.

At the beginning of the nineteenth century, the urgency of restoration measures became obvious given its poor state of preservation. This realization was accompanied by discussion concerning a new installation site, since the surface of the statue was becoming increasingly damaged. In 1873, *David* was finally moved at the decision of an expert committee into the Galleria dell'Accademia (ill. p.62), where it remains on view. Since then a copy of the statue can be seen (ill. p.63) in its previous site in front of the Palazzo Vecchio.

The "tribuna" that was specially designed for *David* by the architect Emilio de Fabris in the Galleria dell'Accademia constitutes an appropriate setting for displaying Michelangelo's giant. Here *David* stands in the center of an apse-like semicircle with a surrounding play of light falling through a glass cupola that arches over it. A further enhancement on the way to viewing *David* was made at the beginning of the nineteenth century through the measures taken by the superintendent at the time, Corrado Ricci, to install Michelangelo's unfinished *Slaves* (ill. p.75), the so-called *Boboli Slaves*, originally created for Pope Julius II's tomb, together with the similarly unfinished figure of *St. Matthew the Apostle* (ill. p.58) in the corridor leading to the "tribuna"—a worthy guard of honor that accompanies the visitor on his way to the giant waiting at the end.

At the end of the twentieth century, the statue underwent extensive investigations. High-ranking science and technology

Copy of *David* on the Piazza della Signoria, in front of the Palazzo Vecchio, placed between Donatello's *Judith and Holofernes* (in the background) and Baccio Bandinelli's *Hercules and Cactus* (in the foreground).

institutes and universities in Italy and the United States analyzed the sculpture's condition of preservation and its surrounding climatic conditions using the latest scientific methods. These included electro-microscopic examinations, as well as infrared photographs of the surface structure, an extremely precise survey of the figure using three-dimensional computer animations, as well as microbiological analyses. These examinations lasted eleven years, in preparation for the restoration measures that followed at the beginning of the twenty-first century, which gave rise to violent disputes between restorers and museum officials. Since opinions differed concerning the restoration method, finally the Italian culture minister himself issued instructions in 2003. In the end, it was decided that the statue should be cleaned with rice-straw paper dipped in distilled water, as well as packs of cellulose and clay, to remove the dirt from the surface. In time for the quincentennial celebrations, in February 2004 Michelangelo's hero then shone with new luster in his place in the Galleria dell'Accademia. Since then a so-called "air-cage" designed by the engineer Livio de Santoli has been protecting the statue from the air pollutants and heat generated by visitors: an ingenious ventilation system is in place to maintain the microclimate around the statue in a constant and pure state.

Michelangelo's biblical hero defies all the debates: the technical mastery of the execution and the beauty and the precision of the anatomy attract the viewer today just as previously it constantly drew contemporaries into its spell. Yet it is above all its symbolic status as a synonym for resolution and the courageous resistance to every threat posed to the freedom and dignity of the human being with which Michelangelo's *David* enters our contemporary age as a messenger.

THE FUNERARY MONUMENT FOR POPE JULIUS II

THE TRAGEDY OF THE TOMB—PART ONE

The sixty-year-old Giuliano della Rovere had already been elected in 1503 as Pope Julius II (ill. p.66). Pius III had previously acceded to the papal throne as Borgia Pope Alexander VI's successor in the same year, but he died on October 18 after only a four-week pontificate. When Julius II took over the papal

Raphael, *Portrait of Pope Julius II*, ca. 1511–12.
Oil on wood, 42½ x 31¾ in. (108 x 80.7 cm). National Gallery, London.

PAGES 64–5
Moses on the tomb for Julius II (detail), 1513–16, final reworking, 1542.
Marble, 92½ in. (235 cm) high.
San Pietro in Vincoli, Rome.

office, the Papal States were in a disastrous state that had been wrought by the rule of Alexander VI and his cruel, murderous son Cesare Borgia. Particularly in the final years of Alexander's pontificate, when his son was de facto ruler of the Papal States, father and son had murdered anyone who dared to stand in the way of their lust for power. After this reign of terror, the new pope from the House of Della Rovere emerged as the true savior of the papacy. He abolished simony and increased the estate to the benefit of the Papal States rather than for his own House. Julius II's strength of purpose is also testified by Raphael's impressive portrait of this pope, a man already well advanced in years; his gaze and bearing reflect this characteristic.

It is uncontested that Julius II ushered in a new period of cultural blossoming and was to prove an important patron in the artistic domain. With the fame of Michelangelo, who was working in Florence, having almost certainly reached his ears, he summoned him to Rome in March 1505 and gave him the commission for a vast funerary monument—that fateful commission that was to feature in Michelangelo's creative work for forty years. It has entered the annals of art history as the *"tragedia della tomba,"* the tragedy of the tomb.

From the outset, the project was dogged by bad luck. This is evidenced by a letter written from Michelangelo, on January 31, 1506, to his father Ludovico in Florence: "As to my affairs here [in Rome], all would be well if my marbles were to come [from Carrara], but as far as this goes I seem to be most unfortunate, for since I arrived here there have not been two days of fine weather. A barge [with marble], which had the greatest luck not to come to grief owing to the bad weather, managed to put in with some of them a few days ago; and then, when I had unloaded them, the river [Tiber] suddenly overflowed its banks and submerged them, so that as yet I haven't been able to begin anything; however, I'm making promises to the pope, and keeping him in a state of agreeable expectation so that he may not be angry with me, in the hope that the weather may clear up so that I can soon begin work—God willing." Michelangelo had previously spent more than eight months in the Carrara

Tomb for Pope Julius II, total view, 1505–45.
Marble. San Pietro in Vincoli, Rome.

66

quarries in order to choose the marble blocks for which he was now waiting desperately. For this he had received a payment of 1000 ducats from the pope. When the marble finally arrived, Michelangelo had it brought to St. Peter's Square, behind Santa Caterina, close to his workshop.

Michelangelo's first design in 1505 planned a vast free-standing tomb based on a rectangular ground plan with sculptural ornamentation of forty figures, which was to be placed in the choir of St. Peter's—in April 1506, Bramante started work on the new construction of the church (ill. p.69). The project—which was never carried out in this form—contained a structure that narrowed in steps leading upward, with the individual stories separated by cornices and subdivided by many niches between which cornice-bearing herms were arranged. On the lower story, statues of captives were to be placed while, for the corners of the first cornice, four sculptures were designed: the figures of *Vita activa* and *Vita contemplativa*, and of *St. Paul* and *Moses*. Friezes and countless decorative elements, as well as bronze reliefs with scenes from the pope's life, were to adorn the tomb, which finished with two figures at the top, "one of which was Heaven, smiling and supporting a bier on her

shoulder, and the other, Cybele, the goddess of the Earth, who appeared to be grief stricken at having to remain in a world robbed of all virtue" (Vasari). Condivi reports that the work was to end "in a surface upon which there were two angels supporting a sarcophagus." The sides of the rectangle were planned to contain door openings that led inside the tomb that was designed in the form of an oval temple, at the center of which would be the pope's sarcophagus.

In early 1506, a quarrel erupted between the pope and Michelangelo. Julius II no longer seemed interested in any continuation of the works on the tomb and ceased to allow Michelangelo any precedence in this matter.

The Michelangelo scholar Antonio Forcellino recently revised the picture of the artist being treated with disregard by the pope and considers a reproachful letter on this subject from Michelangelo that might support the disregard theory instead as another testimony to the artist's habit of adapting the facts to his own advantage. Forcellino, who describes Julius as an extremely patient patron with Michelangelo, regards the pope's behavior instead as an expression of his infuriation with Michelangelo's constant financial demands,

Sketches of the marble blocks for the tomb of Pope Julius II, ca. 1505.
Pen and Indian ink, 8 x 12 in. (20.2 x 30.5 cm). Casa Buonarroti, Florence.

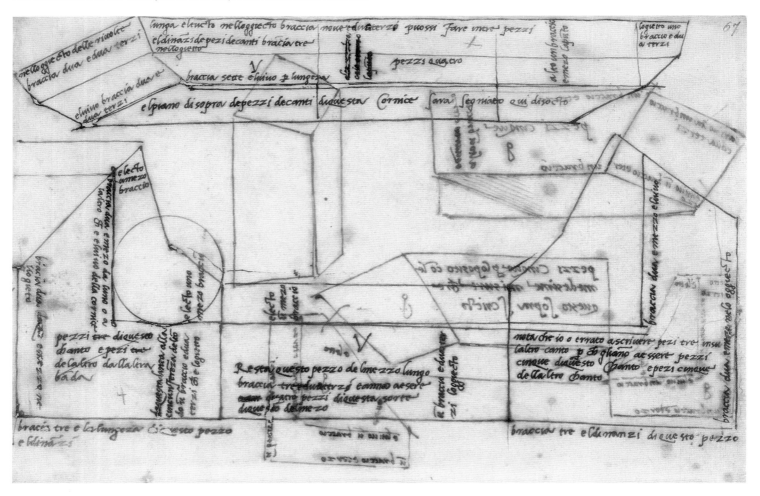

Design for the tomb of Pope Julius II, copy of lost original drawing by
Michelangelo, first project, front view, ca. 1505.
Pen, washes, and red chalk, 11½ x 14¼ in. (29 x 36.1 cm).
Gabinetto dei Disegni e delle Stampe degli Uffizi, Florence.

especially as he was liberally investing the payments he had
received for the marble in Carrara in the acquisition of land.

Michelangelo was certainly high-handed in traveling
away from Rome without the pope's permission—a serious
offense and a highly risky undertaking that also put him
at risk of losing favor with the pope and even being
excommunicated. Over the following three months, in which
Michelangelo stayed in Florence, the pope sent three letters
to the Signoria requesting them to send Michelangelo back to
Rome. Again it was the *gonfalioniere* Piero Soderini who stepped
in as mediator. He persuaded Michelangelo to seek out the
pope and ask for forgiveness and indeed, for protection, as
an envoy of the city. Finally Michelangelo relented and
traveled to Bologna, where the pope was staying for some
political negotiations.

Julius II forgave Michelangelo, but also proposed to him
a new commission to be carried out in Bologna: a larger than
life-size bronze statue of the pope. In 1507, Michelangelo began
the work for this statue, for which he required assistance from
casters, yet the casting threatened to fail: for many months, he
was busy with the final touches and repairs to the cast statue
before it was finally installed over the portal of San Petronio
in Bologna on February 21, 1508. The effigy was not preserved:
during the civil uprising in Bologna against Julius II, the statue
was destroyed on December 30, 1511; the bronze reached the
duke of Ferrara, who had it melted down into a cannon, which
he called "La Giulia."

Michelangelo's quarrel with the pope was settled. After
the completion of the bronze statue, he returned to Rome in
the hope of being able to continue working on the funerary

69

Anastasio Fontebuoni, *Michelangelo before Pope Julius II in Bologna*
(November 1506), 1620–21.
Oil on canvas, 57 x 55½ in. (145 x 141 cm). Casa Buonarroti, Florence.

Fontebuoni's painting depicts the moment at which Michelangelo,
kneeling before the pope, is thought to have asked him for forgiveness.

monument for Julius II. However, nothing came of this. The pope meanwhile had another project in mind—the painting of the ceiling in the Sistine Chapel, built by his uncle, Pope Sixtus IV (1471–84), for which his choice had fallen on Michelangelo.

Michelangelo tried to refuse the commission. He even suggested to the pope his rival Raphael, who had come to Rome in October 1504 and was already very successful at this time. It was to no avail. So he finally accepted the commission; he knew that he could not oppose the pope again. The painting of the Sistine ceiling became the first in a series of monumental commissioned works that were to prevent Michelangelo from continuing work on the Julius funerary monument for the best part of forty years.

THE TRAGEDY OF THE TOMB—PART TWO: THE LONG ROAD TO SAN PIETRO IN VINCOLI

Vasari referred to the "endless vexations and annoyances and drudgery" that dogged Michelangelo throughout the tomb project for Julius II. Michelangelo himself described the Julius tomb as the tragedy of his life: In a letter he sent in October 1542 to Monsignore Aliotti in Rome he complained of having

lost "the whole of my youth" through the work on the funerary monument. The more recent Michelangelo literature even assesses the story of the tomb as "a vast symbol that epitomizes the artistic struggle for survival" (Kupper).

In fact, the challenges of the funerary monument represented possibly the greatest ordeal for Michelangelo as an artist. He found himself at the mercy of various conflicting influences: the shifting interests of the papal rulers, the pressure from the heirs of the House of Della Rovere after the death of his patron Julius II in February 1513, and finally, the political struggle that dominated everything in the context of European states of that period—the struggle between Habsburgs and the French for supremacy in Italy, that was to reach its terrible culmination in 1527 in the Sack of Rome. Five pontificates, from the Della Rovere Pope Julius II (1503–13) to Paul III from the House of Farnese (1534–49) accompanied and influenced the course of the funerary monument until its final installation in San Pietro in Vincoli in 1545 (ill. p.67).

From a contemporary perspective, Michelangelo's strength in overcoming this artistic struggle for survival appears almost superhuman. While Michelangelo was first and foremost under obligation to his ecclesiastical patrons, the popes, after Julius II's death his heirs insisted under the leadership of his nephew Francesco Maria della Rovere, the duke of Urbino, that Michelangelo keep to the contract, which was changed four times in total. Each time was associated with a reduction in the originally vast tomb project. The various versions of the contract in 1505, 1513, and 1516 were followed in 1532 by countless arguments in which Michelangelo was even threatened by Della Rovere with being forced to repay the sum of 16,500 ducats decreed to him in Julius II's will, and finally by an agreement about the final design; this contract had come about through the mediation of Pope Clement VII, who had been in office since 1523. In 1542, it was then modified again. The original conception of the free-standing rectangular tomb had meanwhile been abandoned in favor of a wall-tomb, as had the plan to install it in the new building of St. Peter's; the Julius tomb was to reach its final installation site in the church of San

Dying Captive, ca. 1513–16,
intended for the tomb of Pope Julius II. Marble, 90¼ in. (229 cm) high.
Musée du Louvre, Sculpture Department, Paris.

Bound (Rebellious) Captive, ca. 1513–16,
intended for the tomb of Pope Julius II. Marble, 84¾ in. (215 cm) high.
Musée du Louvre, Sculpture Department, Paris.

Whereas Condivi interpreted the statues of the *Captives* as representations of the liberal arts, in which Michelangelo was indicating that "all the artistic virtues were prisoners of death together with Pope Julius," according to Vasari they represented "all the provinces subjugated by the Pope and made obedient to the Apostolic Church" (Vasari).

Pietro in Vincoli. There in 1533 Michelangelo began with the masonry works. In summer 1543, he was occupied with the final sculptures and the contract agreed to in 1532 was realized up to 1545 in the form of the Julius tomb that can be seen today in San Pietro in Vincoli.

The full import of the scale reduction of the tomb becomes clear only if we recall Michelangelo's first project of 1505, which had planned a figure ornamentation of forty larger than life-size sculptures. In the finally executed version, only seven of these remained, with the figures that are to be seen in the upper story of the tomb—the sibyls, *Madonna and Child*, as well as the prophets by Michelangelo's fellow workers, principally Raffaello da Montelupo—being completed.

The tomb is dominated by the seated figure of Moses placed in the center of the plinth area (ill. p.73). This is among the earliest sculptures carried out for the Julius tomb, just like the statues of *Dying Captive* that can be seen today in the Louvre (ill. p.71) and the unfinished *Bound Captive*, also known as *Rebellious Captive* (ill. p.71); from 1513, Michelangelo worked on the three statues; in 1516, he had largely completed them.

Originally the statues of the *Captives* were intended for installation in the plinth area, in the niches on either side of the *Moses*. In the work on the final version of the tomb, Michelangelo finally decided in 1542 no longer to include them, replacing them with the figures of *Leah* and *Rachel*. In 1546, Michelangelo gave both *Captive* figures to the Florentine Roberto Strozzi in gratitude for the lodging he had given him during two severe illnesses in 1544 and 1545 in his house in Rome. Strozzi, who went into exile in France, then gave them as a present to French King Francis I, and in 1749 they moved to Paris; in 1794 they were acquired by the French state for the Louvre collections, which gave rise to their other name, the *Louvre Captives*.

The Michelangelo literature has shed light on the *Captives* in the context of the discovery of the *Laocoön Group* (ill. p.48), originating from the first century BC, which was excavated in 1506 on the Esquiline Hill in Rome. Michelangelo, who was staying in Giuliano da Sangallo's house in Rome at the time, is supposed to have caught sight of the sculpture himself during its rescue. Specifically, the position of the raised left arm of *Dying Captive* is seen as a reference to the antique group sculpture. While on the one hand the *Captives* represent ideal beauty, as embodiments of the perfect youth figure, on the other hand they speak with great vivacity to the viewer, presenting themselves as people of flesh-and-blood: musculature and bodily build reveal a striving for greater gentleness, demonstrating a departure from the canon of classical forms. This also becomes clearly visible in the individual facial expressions of *Bound Captive*. The form of the youth figures is based on the unique mastery with which Michelangelo worked the marble: it appears not to have been hewn, but rather as stone transformed in the

> "It remained to him to finish the three statues by his own hand, that is, the Moses and two Captives; the which three statues are almost finished. But because the said two Captives were executed when the work was designed to be much larger, and was to include many other statues, which work was afterward in the above-mentioned contract curtailed and reduced; for this reason they are unsuited to the present design, nor would they by any means be appropriate for it. Therefore, the said Messer Michelangelo...began the other statues to go in the same zone as the Moses, the Contemplative Life and the Active."
>
> Michelangelo in a letter of July 20, 1542, to Pope Paul III.

sculptor's hands like a malleable waxen material. It is also clear to see here that the austere bodily profile that characterizes *David* has been overcome.

Vasari gave an excellent description of the *Moses* figure (ill. p.73): "For, seated in an attitude of great dignity, Moses rests one arm on the tablets that he is grasping in one hand, while with the other he is holding his beard, which falls in long ringlets and is carved in the marble so finely that the hairs (extremely difficult for the sculptor to represent) are downy and soft and so detailed that it seems that Michelangelo must have exchanged his chisel for a brush.... In addition, the draperies worn by Moses are carved and finished with beautiful folds in the skirt; and the arms with their muscles and the hands with their bones and tendons are so supremely beautiful, the legs, knees, and feet are covered with such carefully fashioned hose and sandals, and every part of the work is finished so expertly, that today more than ever Moses can truly be called the friend of God."

Michelangelo revised the figure of *Moses* in 1542 after he became dissatisfied with the posture he designed in his first sketch. The figure seems to tremble with energetic tension: It is easy to imagine that the proclaimer of God's laws described in the Old Testament is on the very point of jumping up and,

▷ *Moses* from the tomb for Pope Julius II, 1513–16, final reworking, 1542. Marble, 92½ in. (235 cm) high. San Pietro in Vincoli, Rome.

The two horns on the head of *Moses* are due incidentally to a mistranslation of the original text in the "Vulgate," which characterized the representation of Moses from the twelfth century; what was originally meant were rays (2 Moses 34, 29), as signs of Moses' inspiration.

angry with the unbelieving Israelites, smashing the tablets with the Ten Commandments. Here, too, we are confronted with a figure that in its kinetic dynamism conveys to the viewer that transitory moment or state of tension that precedes the approaching events, as we have already observed in *David*.

Claudia Echinger-Maurach (1991) also sees in the kinetic energy revealed in the formation of the limbs a connection with the figures of the Sistine Chapel ceiling: like *Libyan Sibyl* (ill. p.4) or the prophet *Jonah* (ill. pp.118–19) that are portrayed there, *Moses* wears "instead of a robe and coat only a shirt that molds to the muscular upper body.... It is only the energy of the movement that pushes and layers the fabric of the garments around the limbs, as if the figure becomes smaller as a result... for the splendor of the individual limbs is emphasized."

In the period from 1519 to 1525, when Michelangelo was already working under commission from Pope Leo X on the Medici graves in San Lorenzo, he also created more statues for the Julius tomb: *Bearded Slave* (ill. p.76), *Awakening Slave* (ill. p.75), *Young Slave*, and *Atlas Slave*. The four figures that Michelangelo had intended for installation in the first story of the tomb were never included in the entire tomb composition and they all remained unfinished. They are also known as the *Boboli Slaves*, since Duke Cosimo I, who received the sculptures after Michelangelo's death from his nephew Lionardo, had them installed as decoration in a cave in the Boboli Gardens; in 1908, they moved to the Accademia, also in Florence.

As previously with the *Louvre Captives*, Michelangelo liberates these figures from the classical canon of forms: the bodies have great vivacity, the turning movements of the upper body, the arms clasped over the head, and the bent legs give

the figures remarkable dynamism. Moreover, Michelangelo's technique becomes clearly visible in the figures. Details such as the head of *Bearded Slave* reveal how he placed the chisel and, beyond this, the figures show how he worked out from the stone the bodies that were already contained in it—according to his *concetto*—working out individual parts perfectly while leaving others rough-hewn.

Whether Michelangelo created the figure of *Victor*, also known as *Victory* (ill. p.77), in the 1519–25 period as well, cannot to this day be clearly determined; it is established in some of the research as originating between 1532 and 1534. The powerful serpentine line of the bodily posture and the lively musculature, including that of the upper body, are striking, and stylistically they place the figure within the ornamental sculpture series of the Medici graves in San Lorenzo (see ill. pp.128–9). The pose of the young victor, who presses his left leg on the back of the enemy who is forced to kneel below him, is also reminiscent of *David*: there is no triumphant

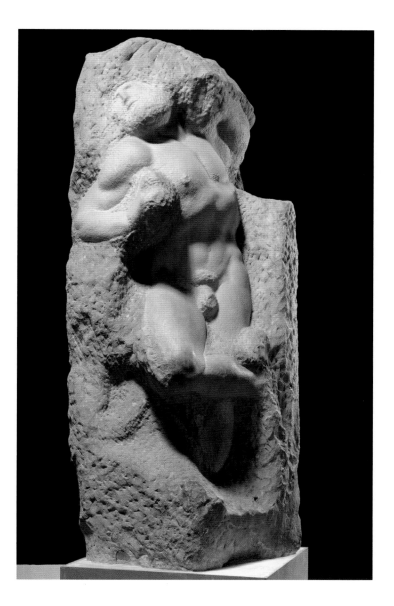

▷ *Awakening Slave*, ca. 1519–ca. 1530.
Marble, 109 in. (277 cm) high, unfinished.
Galleria dell'Accademia, Florence.

The figures of *Awakening Slave* and *Bearded Slave* belong, together with *Young Slave* and *Atlas Slave*, to the four so-called *Boboli Slaves*, which were designed for the tomb of Pope Julius II.

◁ *Moses* from the tomb for Pope Julius II (detail of the right torso area with arm supported on the tablet of the laws), 1513–16, final reworking, 1542. San Pietro in Vincoli, Rome.

PAGE 76
Bearded Slave, ca. 1519–ca. 1530.
Marble, 102¾ in. (261 cm) high, unfinished.
Galleria dell'Accademia, Florence.

PAGE 77
Victor (Victory), ca. 1519–34.
Marble, 102¾ in. (261 cm) high.
Palazzo Vecchio, Florence.

Tomb for Pope Julius II, 1505–45. Marble. San Pietro in Vincoli, Rome.

The recumbent figure of the pope is thought to have been executed by Tommaso di Pietro Boscoli (Maso del Bosco). It is flanked on the left by a sibyl and on the right by a prophet, both of which were executed by Raffaello da Montelupo. The *Madonna and Child* is by Domenico Fancelli.

quality to *Victor* either. His countenance testifies to the rational purpose of the Renaissance hero who is master of his destiny; his facial expressions reflect that restrained energy and intellectual tension that also inhabit Michelangelo's biblical hero.

The female figures of *Leah* and *Rachel* (ill. pp.80, 81) in the niches on either side of Moses in the plinth area, the embodiments of the active and the contemplative life—the *vita activa* and the *vita contemplativa*—were intended by Michelangelo in his first plan of 1505 for the Julius tomb; they were to be placed on the "corners of the first cornice" (Vasari). Yet Michelangelo sculpted these figures only from 1542, so they actually originated during the final completion phase of the tomb.

The head of *Leah* standing to Moses' left, also a symbol of *caritas*, Christian charity, is slightly inclined to one side and she is looking ahead in a peaceful contemplative attitude; in her right hand, she is holding an oil lamp of which the flame is being fed from her hair. Burning hair was considered in medieval tradition to be a sign of the benevolent thoughts that lead to *caritas*. *Rachel*, also a symbol of belief, turns her countenance to the sky, with her hands folded in prayer in front of her chest.

Both figures radiate a great gentleness and spiritual peace that are new in Michelangelo's figure composition.

> *"Let it suffice that this is all I deserve in return for thirty-six years of fair dealing and ungrudging devotion to others. Painting and sculpture, hard work, and fair dealing have been my ruin and things go continually from bad to worse. It would have been better had I been put to making matches in my youth, than to be in such a fret!"*
>
> *Michelangelo in a letter to his friend Luigi del Riccio in Rome, shortly before October 24, 1542.*

In this respect, they also constitute the polar opposite to the turmoil and energetic quality of the figure of *Moses* that he originally created in 1513–16. In the facial expressions and gestures of the female figures is revealed a stylistic change that can be considered an expression of a new spirituality, which Michelangelo discovered largely through the influence of his friend Vittoria Colonna and the circle of the Catholic reform movement of the "Spirituali," as we will also see in his late work.

There is some dispute concerning the assessment of the recumbent figure of the pope in the middle of the upper story (ill. pp.78–9), which also originated in the final phase of work on the Julius tomb of 1541 to 1545. Vasari already mentions that the figure was not worked by Michelangelo himself but by

of the pope's hands. In the established tradition, the blessing or resting gesture of the hands was characteristic of statues of the pope; this can be seen, for example, in the tombs made by Antonio del Pollaiuolo for Sixtus IV (completed in 1493) and his successor Innocent VIII (completed in 1498, the year of Pollaiuolo's death) in St. Peter's Church.

To Forcellino, the hands here seem to testify to defeat, the "awareness of the futility and vanity of human actions, which have no bearing on eternity." The renunciation of any sumptuous regalia and the usual tokens of magnificent display for the glorification of the pope also manifests, according to Forcellino, a new feeling: "that in fact the church should find its way back to a purely spiritual dimension, far away from the exercise of worldly power and the heinous dealings carried out in its name."

Against the background of the increasingly powerful Inquisition in the 1540s and the reorganizational endeavors of the Catholic Church following the Council of Trent (1545–63), this clear attitude is revolutionary. Even Forcellino takes the view that this image of the pope could "probably scarcely" have been produced without the agreement of the patrons, Julius II's heirs from the House of Della Rovere.

The "tragedy of the tomb" that had plagued Michelangelo's conscience in over four decades of quarrels and wrestling with the Della Rovere family came to an end with the completion of the Julius tomb in 1545. In the final version, all that remained of the original design was a torso, which is influenced by the impact of the all-dominating figure of Moses; this even inspired Sigmund Freud to make a detailed study. Here explicit reference should also be made to Claudia Echinger-Maurach's extensive 1991 study, which contains new insights concerning the Julius tomb.

the sculptor Maso del Bosco. This view is shared in the earlier Michelangelo literature, such as by the great art historians Charles de Tolnay and Erwin Panofsky. It is therefore surprising to encounter the certainty with which the Michelangelo scholar Antonio Forcellino describes the pope figure as the master's own "compositional masterpiece," stating that Michelangelo had allowed only the legs to be executed by an assistant. Forcellino bases his evaluation specifically on Michelangelo's inspired stratagem for integrating the figure into the narrow architectonic space, as well as the convincing production of the illusion of movement.

Whether in fact the pope figure originates from Michelangelo's hand or not, there is a noteworthy detail that demonstrates an innovation in the iconography—the posture

PAGE 80
Leah (Vita activa) from the tomb for Pope Julius II, ca. 1542–45.
Marble, 82¼ in. (209 cm) high.
San Pietro in Vincoli, Rome.

PAGE 81
Rachel (Vita contemplativa) from the tomb for Pope Julius II, ca. 1542–45.
Marble, 77½ in. (197 cm) high.
San Pietro in Vincoli, Rome.

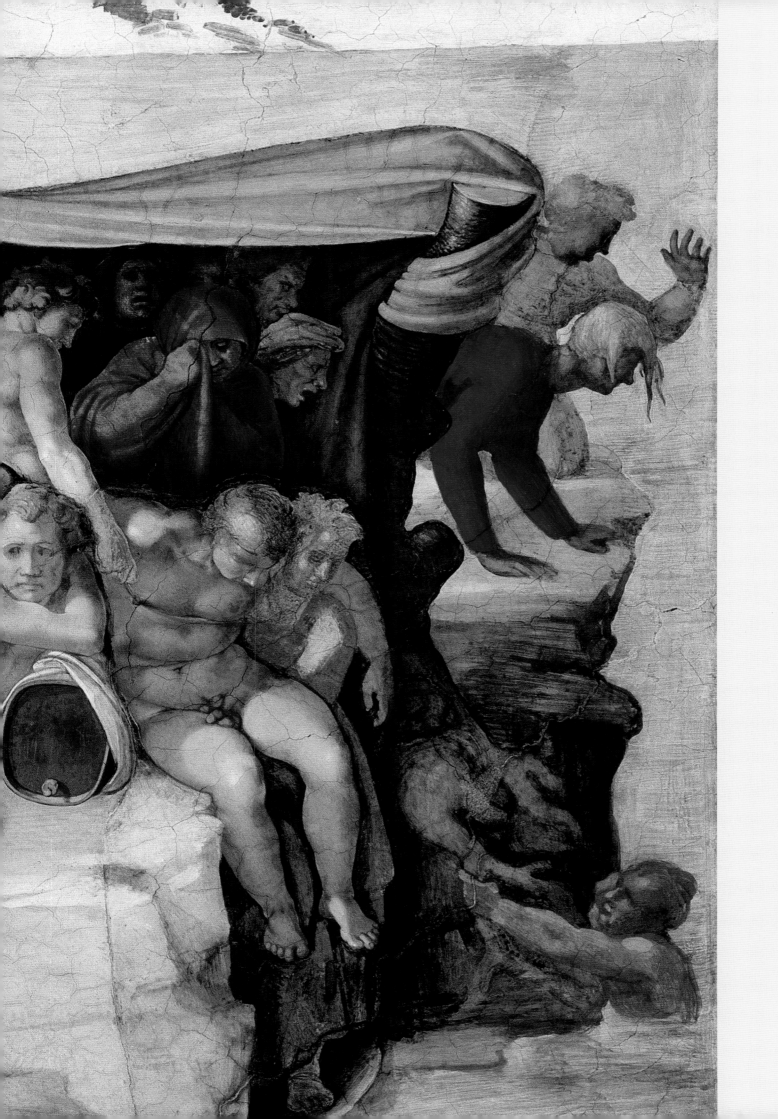

THE VAULT FRESCOES OF THE SISTINE CHAPEL

"...THIS IS NOT MY ART"

"...until you have seen the Sistine Chapel, you have no adequate conception of what man is capable of accomplishing. One hears and reads of so many great and worthy people, but here, above one's head and before one's eyes, is living evidence of what *one* man has done" (Goethe). This is how Goethe describes the overwhelming impression made on him by Michelangelo's painting of the Sistine Chapel (ill. p.85) on August 23, 1787, in his travel diary, *The Italian Journey*. Goethe's feeling, recorded 275 years after the completion of the frescoes in 1512, accords with the reaction of Michelangelo's contemporaries, including his famous fellow artist and rival Raphael, who all fell silent at the monumentality of the ceiling paintings when they were unveiled. While scarcely ten years earlier Michelangelo had already won extraordinary fame with *David*, which earned him preeminence as the foremost marble sculptor in Italy, with the Sistine ceiling at the age of only thirty-seven years he was to become a legend; in painting Michelangelo set new standards against which every artist had to allow himself to be measured.

On May 8, 1508, he had signed the contract with Pope Julius II, assuring him a fee of 3000 ducats. Michelangelo had been extremely reluctant to accept this commission, and he was rightly afraid that this vast undertaking after his return to Rome at the end of March 1508 would ruin his further work on the marble blocks for the Julius mausoleum. The suggestion that the idea of commissioning Michelangelo had been put into the pope's head by the court architect Bramante in order to destroy his unpleasant rival's capacity to undertake any further sculptural works and thus his high regard with the pope—as Michelangelo later implied through his biographers Vasari and Condivi—was later banished from the Michelangelo literature into the realm of myth-making. This recognition is based primarily on a letter written on May 10, 1506, by Michelangelo's friend Piero Rosselli, who was later to collaborate with him in the construction of the painting scaffold and the plastering during the preparation of the walls. Rosselli's letter proves that Julius II already cherished the plan to commission Michelangelo in 1506 and, moreover, describes details of a discussion Bramante had with the pope. The doubt expressed there by Bramante as to whether it was wise to commission Michelangelo, who had limited experience in fresco painting, for such a vast project, was cleared by the Michelangelo expert Antonio Forcellino of the criticism of pure hostility and judged to be an objection based on sound common sense. Furthermore, this was to prove well-founded, for in fact Michelangelo had to solve some difficult technical problems in the first phase of work on the Sistine ceiling.

Piero Rosselli first constructed the scaffold designed by Michelangelo. A preserved pen sketch by Michelangelo gives us an idea of its ingenious construction (ill. pp.86–7). Michelangelo had rejected the scaffold structure previously devised by Bramante that planned to anchor a hanging platform in the side walls of the chapel—raising the problem of perforation of the vault. Michelangelo's scaffold, which had to be more than 65 feet (20 meters) high and required the bridging of a space more than 50 feet (16 meters) wide, consisted of a central platform resting on wooden supports so that the masonry was not touched. It enabled Michelangelo to paint the ceiling zones of the middle section of the vault either sitting or lying down; steps on either side enabled him to paint the vaulted ceiling zone as well as the severies, and from another platform at the base of the scaffold, he was able to paint the lunettes on the side walls over the window areas. Sailcloth tarpaulins were fixed under the scaffold to prevent the color falling onto the marble floor of the chapel. The flawless scaffold construction afforded a broad free passage for the Masses and ceremonies that continued to be held during the painting in the chapel.

Michelangelo had meanwhile commissioned his friend Francesco Granacci, with whom he had already worked in the Ghirlandaios' workshop in Florence, to hire collaborators in Florence for his project. The painters engaged by Granacci

PAGES 82–3
The Flood (detail), 1508–09.
Fresco, 110¼ x 224½ in. (280 x 570 cm).
Vatican, Sistine Chapel, Rome.

Sistine Chapel, with west-facing view of altar wall with *The Last Judgment*, and in the middle section of the side walls the painting series with scenes from *The Life of Moses* and *The Life of Christ* that originated under Pope Sixtus IV.

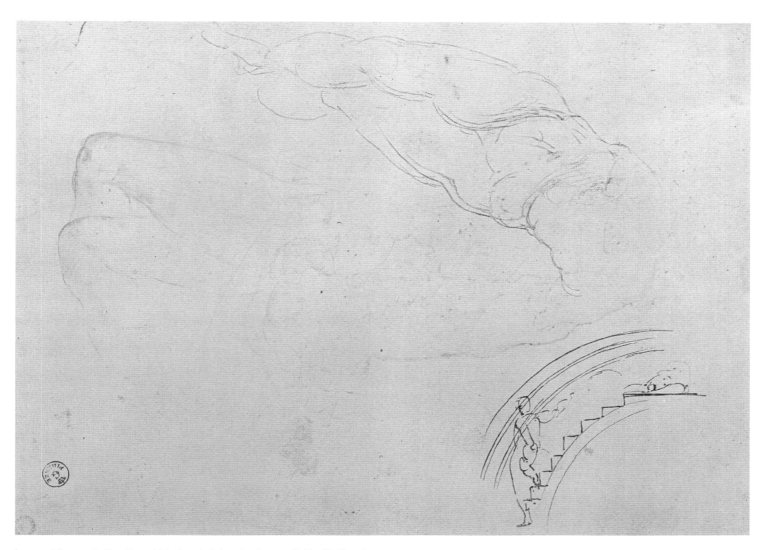

Leg and figure studies thought to be sketches for the scaffold with the steps
at the side designed for the painting of the Sistine Chapel,
ca. 1508(?). Pen, red chalk, black chalk, silverpoint, 10 x 13¾ in. (25.5 x
35 cm). Gabinetto dei Disegni e delle Stampe degli Uffizi, Florence.

affair" to portray only the apostles, he had communicated this
to the pope, who then—according to Michelangelo—gave him
a completely free hand with the design. By scholars, however,
it has unanimously been doubted that Michelangelo had sole
responsibility for the iconographic program.

Since there is no available evidence documenting Julius
II's intentions concerning the iconographic program, nor
any extant written notes by Michelangelo about his project,
research to this day has made various conjectures about the
decisive influences on the iconographic program. In this
context, the names that emerge are the respected papal advisor
and theologian Egidio da Viterbo, who had studied with the
Augustinians and was seeking to bring the antique world into
accordance with Christian tradition and Catholic doctrine
and, furthermore, had a very good knowledge of Neoplatonic
philosophy, and the Franciscan Marco Vigerio, who promoted
Julius II to cardinal. The doctrines of St. Bonaventura and
St. Augustine are also adduced as theological sources. While

this background also leaves some divergence in the
interpretative endeavors, there is nevertheless a consensus in
research that underlying the layers of meaning in the frescoes
is "a system of calculated symmetries and correspondences"
that developed in the course of a century-old interpretative
tradition of the Holy Scriptures (De Vecchi).

The narrative structure of the central ceiling pictures thus
reflects the Renaissance thinking that the events in Christian
history follow a linear development according to a divine plan
that will continue until the end of time. Michelangelo thus
created the scenes in reverse chronological order, beginning
at the chapel entrance and leading up to the altar. He
accomplished *Division of Light from Darkness* on the first day
of the Creation story as the last of the nine episodes (see
ill. pp.90–91 and Sistine Chapel fold-out).

The central section of the ceiling consists of nine picture
zones from the first book of Moses, Genesis; this represents the
"core meaning" of Michelangelo's iconographic program (Beck).

Together with the scenes from the lives of Moses and Christ that appear in the twelve picture zones on the side walls under the window zones, Michelangelo's Genesis scenes, which depict the world before the judgment, complete the traditional Christian three-stage view of history. The scenes of Moses and Christ had already been created from 1481 by Perugino, Domenico Ghirlandaio, Sandro Botticelli, Cosimo Rosselli, Luca Signorelli, and their assistants under commission from Julius II's uncle, Pope Sixtus IV (1471–84), who had had the chapel named after him built from 1477 to 1480.

The nine episodes in the ceiling zones of the middle section are bordered by a painted marble cornice that is borne by pairs of putti. Each individual scene is again framed by four naked young boys, the *ignudi*, sitting on painted plinths (ill. pp.90–91). They are holding medallions with scenes from the books of Genesis, Samuel, Kings, and Maccabees, as well as garlands of oak leaves and oaks. The nine picture zones, of varying size, depict events from the Book of Genesis, including six episodes from the Creation: *Division of Light from Darkness* (ill. pp.90–91), *Creation of Sun, Moon, and Plants, Separation of the Waters from the Sky* (ill. pp.94–5), *Creation of Adam* (ill. pp.96, 98–9), *Creation of Eve* (ill. p.97), *The Fall and Expulsion from Paradise* (ill. pp.100–101), as well as three scenes from the life of Noah: *Noah's Thanks Offering* (ill. pp.102–103), *The Flood* (ill. pp.106–107), and *Drunkenness of Noah* (ill. pp.104–105); they illustrate the origin of humanity, the Fall, the reconciliation with God, and the promise of a future redemption.

In the eight spandrels on the side walls and the lunettes over the windows on the long sides of the chapel, Michelangelo represented Christ's ancestors, as well as four events from the history of the Jewish people in the corner pendentives: *Judith and Holofernes, David and Goliath* (ill. p.111), *Brazen Serpent* (ill. p.110), and *Punishment of Haman*. In the spandrels between the side pendentives appear the twelve immense figures of the seven prophets seated on their thrones and the five sibyls (ill. p.112).

In summer 1508, the preparatory works were so near completion that Michelangelo was able to begin work on the central ceiling zones with his colleagues from Florence. It is regarded as certain today that they began with the fresco of *The Flood* (ill. pp.82–3, 106–107). In the course of the work on this picture zone a first crisis occurred that justified the doubts expressed by Bramante. Both Condivi and Vasari report the problem that the fresco of *The Flood*, scarcely completed, began to go moldy and the figures had therefore become almost indiscernible. Michelangelo is supposed as a result to have gone to see the pope—he still cherished hopes of being released from the commission by this failure: "Indeed I told Your Holiness that this is not my art; what I have done is spoiled. And if you do not believe it, send someone to see" (Condivi).

The pope consequently sent Giuliano da Sangallo to Michelangelo; it was Sangallo who gave the crucial advice to change the proportions of Roman china clay and Travertine

chalk for the plaster, which behaves differently from the mixture of chalk and sand that was used in Florence. A further problem consisted in the application of *a secco* painting, in which Michelangelo used distempers that he applied to the dry plaster rather than, as in *buon fresco* (in good fresco technique), to the damp plaster; these were lacking in durability.

The fiasco of *The Flood* demonstrated the stringent requirements of the fresco technique: corrections were impossible to make on the plaster once it had hardened. The subsequent restoration works also showed that large areas of the already painted work had broken off and been newly painted. Furthermore, during this work phase in the severe winter of 1509, which exposed Michelangelo and his colleagues to the harshest physical conditions, there were considerable tensions with the

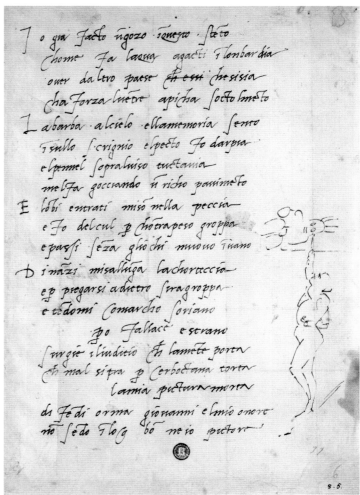

Sketchbook page with Michelangelo's sonnet to Giovanni Benedetto da Pistoia about his painting works on the ceiling fresco of the Sistine Chapel ca. 1509 or ca. 1511–12(?).
Pen, 11¼ x 7¾ in. (28.3 x 20 cm).
Archivio Buonarroti, Florence.

G. Tognetti, Reconstruction of the Sistine Chapel interior in the time of Sixtus IV before Michelangelo's painting; in the vault, Piero Matteo d'Amelia's painting of a starlit sky can still be seen.

assistants, following which the first thing Michelangelo did in January 1509 was to dismiss his assistant, Jacopo di Sandro.

In a letter to his father on January 27, 1509, in which Michelangelo complained about his dissatisfaction with the progress of the work, which was not his "métier," he also discussed Jacopo's dismissal and warned his father not to believe the grievances that could be anticipated from Jacopo on his return to Florence: "Turn a deaf ear and leave it at that." His annoyance about his "dead painting" was also given expression in a sonnet addressed to Giovanni Benedetto da Pistoia that Michelangelo penned in calligraphy on a sketchbook page— next to it he drew a figure painting a vault (ill. p.89)—and in which he made sarcastic complaints about the strains of the painting works.

The technical difficulties were finally overcome, a good quality was achieved for the plaster, and the proportion of *a secco* painting was clearly reduced. Thus the restoration works that were completed in 1994 also showed that in fact only a few parts were carried out in *a secco* painting. It is clearly visible on the painting of the central ceiling zones that from the fourth scene, the episode with *The Fall and Expulsion from Paradise*, Michelangelo was acquiring increasing technical and representational mastery; he reduced the number of figures, increased their size, and gave the compositions more clarity. He also broke away from the dusting-through technique here for the first time and instead engraved the patterns onto the plaster. Later, for example with the execution of the lunettes, he completely abandoned the preliminary cartoons and painted the subject directly onto the background. His technical virtuosity and painterly perfection so increased that, in the parts that originated later, the boundaries of the painting sections of each day's work, the *giornate*, became almost invisible and fused into one homogeneous whole.

In August 1510, Michelangelo had completed with his assistants the first part of the ceiling painting with the fresco of *The Fall and Expulsion from Paradise*. However, at the beginning of September he had to interrupt the work. In a letter dated September 5, 1510, to his father Ludovico, Michelangelo complained not only about his outstanding fee of 500 ducats which he had been promised for the second part of the painting, but also the absence of the pope, who had apparently traveled away without leaving any instructions for him, "so that I find myself without any money and do not know what I ought to do." In fact it was only after the pope had had sight of the work already completed that Michelangelo obtained his agreement to continue work in fall 1510. The scaffold was reerected in the area of the vault over the altar wall. In this second major phase of work followed the fresco-painting of the vault until October 1512. The enormity of Michelangelo's achievement becomes clear if we consider that in only four more years he had painted an enormous surface of 1200 square meters in total with approximately 300 figures.

The restoration works shed light on many questions about Michelangelo's working method, in particular the application of paint and the painting technique. However, the complexity of the iconographic program and the layers of meaning in the Sistine ceiling have eluded entirely conclusive analysis to this day. Thus, details of the representation, for example in the scenes depicted on the bronze medallions or the bronze nudes, the *nudi bronzei*, in the vault corners on either side of the ram's skull have not been convincingly interpreted to this day. From the wealth of the iconographic program a few small scenes should be selected here as examples that primarily reveal the innovations made by Michelangelo in the representation of the subject.

Let us first direct our gaze to the image of God. He appears in five scenes in total on the ceiling. If we follow this in its chronology of origination, we see in *Creation of Eve* (ill. p.97) the ceiling zone in the center of the vault, the massive figure of God the Father standing on the ground, who with the gesture of His right hand seems almost to be beckoning Eve out of Adam; his facial expression is pensive, like that of a

Division of Light from Darkness, 1511.
Fresco, 70¾ x 102¼ in. (180 x 260 cm).
Left the *ignudi* over *Prophet Jeremiah*, 1511.
Fresco, 78¾ x 155½ in. (200 x 395 cm).
Right the *ignudi* over *Libyan Sibyl*, 1511.
Fresco, 76¾ x 151½ in. (195 x 385 cm). Vatican, Sistine Chapel, Rome.

concerned *paterfamilias*. Only here God is depicted peacefully, whereas in the other scenes he is portrayed extremely dynamically and floating freely in the air. Thus, in *Creation of Adam* (ill. p.96) God appears as a spiritual force—He moves with tremendous speed through the air and breathes life into Adam, created in His own image. In *Division of Light from Darkness* (ill. pp.90–91), the titanic figure of God is shown from below in a spiral turning movement with arms thrown high. The garments of God the Father seem to fuse with the powerful gust of air that surrounds Him; the boundaries between material and the surrounding space seem to blur; the representation already appears almost Expressionist in its abstract design.

A fundamental innovation with which Michelangelo anticipated later artistic developments emerges in the depiction of the human being in the principal scenes. He portrays them as real people in their animality and vitality, but also in their subjection to the powers placed over them. In their humanity, Michelangelo's protagonists speak directly to the viewer. Antonio Forcellino described Michelangelo's picture narratives as hymns to physical existence that are clearly distinguished from the strict, static descriptions of the scenes from the lives of Christ and Moses that Michelangelo's famous fellow artists had portrayed on the side walls of the chapel. Michelangelo not only depicted the human being that God created in His own image; but also the other, the animal, side of His nature. This can be seen very impressively on the fifth ceiling picture, which reveals a diptych structure, uniting two scenes with *The Fall* on one side (ill. p.100) and *Expulsion from Paradise* on the other (ill. p.101). In *The Fall*, Eve appears lying on the ground, looking seductively beautiful; she is waiting for the Devil in the form of a snake with a female body to give her the apple, while Adam tries to pick the forbidden fruits.

In *Expulsion*, in which the angel appears with his sword, pain and despair show in Adam's face. In a crouching posture, Eve has visibly aged; her face that was so beautiful before appears to have been distorted into an ugly grimace. Alexander Stützer has poignantly analyzed the ugliness here as a consequence of guilt (Stützer).

In the ceiling fresco with the most figures, *The Flood*, the expressions of human feeling emerge perhaps most clearly of all (ill. pp.106–107). The picture, completed in twenty-nine working days, was severely damaged in 1797 by a gunpowder explosion in the Borgo Sant'Angelo that caused large parts of the plaster to fall off, as can still be observed today. The picture is divided into three thematic areas. In the left half of the picture is a rising desolate hill with a windblown tree on which a crowd of people with all their belongings are seeking rescue from the deluge of water, while in the middle of the picture

The *ignudi* over *Prophet Daniel*, 1511.
Fresco, 76¾ x 151½ in. (195 x 385 cm).
Detail of *Separation of the Waters from the Sky* (see pp.94–5).

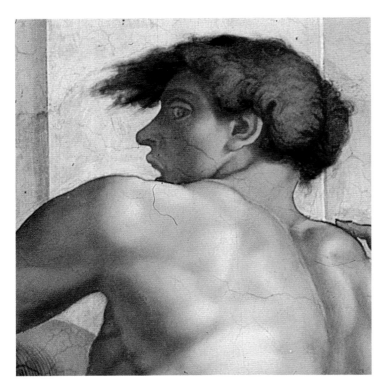

Separation of the Waters from the Sky, 1511.
Fresco, 61 x 106¼ in. (155 x 270 cm).
Left the *ignudi* over *Persian Sibyl*, 1511.
Fresco, 78¾ x 155½ in. (200 x 395 cm).
Right the *ignudi* over *Prophet Daniel*, 1511.
Fresco, 76¾ x 151½ in. (195 x 385 cm).
Vatican, Sistine Chapel, Rome.

The right *ignudo* over *Persian Sibyl* (detail above) and the left *ignudo* over *Prophet Daniel* (detail, pp. 92–3) are highly impressive examples of Michelangelo's unique ingenuity: Through their different bodily postures and their varied facial expressions, the youth figures give expression to a wide range of emotions.

Creation of Adam, 1510. Fresco, 102¼ x 224½ in. (260 x 570 cm).
Vatican, Sistine Chapel, Rome.

many figures are struggling wildly for their lives in a boat that resembles an enormous washtub on the point of sinking. Behind this appears the palatial-looking Noah's ark, on which some people have escaped the deluge and saved their lives. The right side of the picture contains a cliff rising out of the water on which people are seeking refuge under a makeshift tent construction. The people show a variety of forms of behavior and emotional states: "For in the heads of these figures one sees life in prey to death, along with fear, dismay, and hopelessness. Michelangelo also showed the pious actions of many people who are helping one another to climb to safety to the top of a rock. Among them is a man who has clasped someone who is half dead and is striving his utmost to save him; and nothing better than this could be seen in living nature" (Vasari). In the center, however, stands the theme of rescue, which is not only symbolized by the ark as the image of the holy church, but also is illustrated by countless individual figures: the woman with the over-inflated coat who is holding her child tightly clasped, the strong man who is carrying a young woman on his back slightly uphill and the old man on the left in front of the rocky island, who is carrying a young man whom he has presumably

After Michelangelo, *Recumbent Male Nude*, study for
Creation of Adam, ca. 1510(?).
Red chalk, chalk, 7½ x 10 in. (19 x 25.7 cm).
British Museum, London.

THE CEILING FRESCOES
OF THE SISTINE CHAPEL

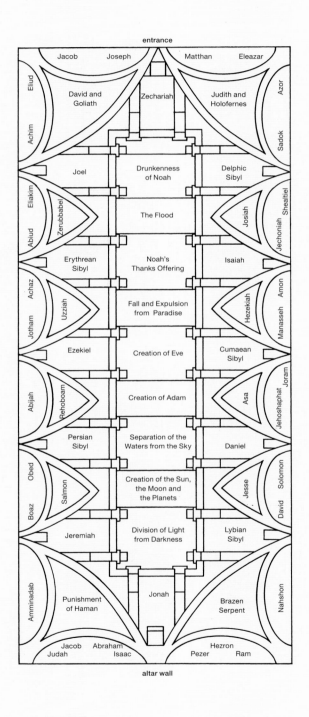

entrance

| Jacob | Joseph | | Matthan | Eleazar |

Eliud

David and Goliath   Zechariah   Judith and Holofernes

Azor

Achim

Sadok

Joel   Drunkenness of Noah   Delphic Sibyl

Eliakim

Zerubbabel   The Flood   Josiah

Jechoniah Sheatiel

Abiud

Erythrean Sibyl   Noah's Thanks Offering   Isaiah

Achaz

Uzziah   Fall and Expulsion from Paradise   Hezekiah

Amon Manasseh

Jotham

Ezekiel   Creation of Eve   Cumaean Sibyl

Abijah

Rehoboam   Creation of Adam   Asa

Joram Jehoshaphat

Persian Sibyl   Separation of the Waters from the Sky   Daniel

Obed

Salmon   Creation of the Sun, the Moon and the Planets   Jesse

Solomon David

Boaz

Jeremiah   Division of Light from Darkness   Lybian Sibyl

Amminadab

Punishment of Haman   Jonah   Brazen Serpent

Nahshon

| Jacob | Abraham | Hezron | |
| Judah | Isaac | Pezer | Ram |

altar wall

▷ *Erythraean Sibyl*, 1509, fresco,
149½ x 141¾ in. (380 x 360 cm), Rome, Vatican, Sistine Chapel.

INSIDE
Full view of the ceiling frescoes of the Sistine Chapel

◁ Right *ignudo* of the *ignudi* pair over the *Delphic Sibyl*, 1509, fresco, Rome, Vatican, Sistine Chapel.

Garments study for the *Erythraean Sibyl*, circa 1508, black chalk, pen, dark brown Indian ink over brown brush strokes, 15¼ x 10¼ in. (38.7 x 26 cm), London, British Museum

Creation of Eve, ca. 1509–10. Fresco, 67 x 102¼ in. (170 x 260 cm). Vatican, Sistine Chapel, Rome.

PAGES 98–9
Creation of Adam (detail). Vatican, Sistine Chapel, Rome.

saved from drowning. James Beck has interpreted this pair of figures as a "poignant paraphrase of constant struggle," through which Michelangelo also alluded to his own struggle with the decoration of the ceiling vault, and the superhuman endeavors involved, and thus introduced a personal level of meaning into the picture story (Beck).

Also in the sixteen lunettes (ill. p.108 and Sistine Chapel fold-out), as well as the severies over them on the side walls of the chapel (ill. p.109 and Sistine Chapel fold-out), in which Michelangelo portrayed Christ's ancestors, he managed to depict completely different existential situations and a vast abundance of human emotional states. The lunettes, indicated according to antique tradition with nameplates through which the figures can be identified, are devoted to the family theme, the representation of parents and children. They symbolize the world before the judgment in the anticipation of Christ's coming. The lunettes are structured in two halves, in one of which appear female figures, such as a mother with her children—an implicit reference to the Madonna and Child theme; in the other are male figures. While the male figures look pensive and despondent, even melancholic, the female figures exhibit

steadiness and peace, as well as a deep relationship with their children. In Renaissance painting, this level of detail in the representation of parents and children is unique. An innovation that Michelangelo introduced into the representation is shown in the *Salmon, Boaz, Obed* lunette (ill. p.108 top), in which the left side depicts Ruth, who has just breastfed her son Obed—her exposed breast has only been visible again since the restoration—while on the right an old man with a pilgrim's staff can be seen. The idea that the old man represented in profile with the protruding long white beard shows the biblical figure of Boaz is not considered certain in research. The old man is looking angrily into his own distorted image in the knob of the pilgrim's staff—a grotesque iconographic element that, as the Michelangelo scholar Carl Justi has already indicated, is alien to the Italian painting of the period. Essential here, however, is the opposition between the psychological expressions of the figures: the mother's solicitude and calm is juxtaposed with the "aggressive self-assurance" of the old man (Kupper).

Vasari and Condivi praised the variety of the movements and the diverse postures of the figures in the vault frescoes. In the naked youth-figures of the *ignudi*, this is impressive to

PAGES 100–101
The Fall and Expulsion from Paradise, ca. 1509–10.
Fresco, 110¼ x 224½ in. (280 x 570 cm).
Vatican, Sistine Chapel, Rome.

PAGES 102–103
Noah's Thanks Offering, 1509.
Fresco, 67 x 102¼ in. (170 x 260 cm).
Left *ignudi* pair over *Erythraean Sibyl*.
Fresco, 75¾ x 153½ in. (190 x 390 cm).
Right *ignudi* pair over *Prophet Isaiah*.
Fresco, 74¾ x 155½ in. (190 x 395 cm).
Vatican, Sistine Chapel, Rome.

Drunkenness of Noah, ca. 1509.
Fresco, 67 x 102¼ in. (170 x 260 cm).
Vatican, Sistine Chapel, Rome.

observe. Here Michelangelo both demonstrated his sculptural origins and in the nude painting engaged with antique sculptures, while also honing his skill in representing human anatomy. Despite their masculinity and the almost Herculean powers that they radiate, the *ignudi* are to be interpreted as angels, embodiments of the divine spirit and at the same time God's servants, chosen to testify to the earliest stage of human history. They are captured in very different movements and bodily attitudes, one resting and the other full of dynamism. The two *ignudi* over *Prophet Jeremiah* (ill. pp.90–91) bear witness to the perfection of Michelangelo's mastery of nude painting: While the left *ignudo* sits extremely gracefully leaning back on his marble plinth, his companion on the right is characterized by a complicated turning movement of the body, emphasized to the utmost, which seems to be inspired by *Belvedere Torso* (see figure in Chronology fold-out). One detail of the *ignudo* with the headband should be emphasized: the bundle of oaks on which the youth is resting his right arm. The oaks contain a play on the family name of Pope Julius II, Della Rovere (of the oak). What is striking is the resemblance of the oaks, considered to be fertility symbols, to the phallus of the *ignudo*. James Beck regarded this as "an inside joke or burla," a humorous reference to the patron (Beck).

The diversity of emotions in the *ignudi* testifies to Michelangelo's ingenuity, if we consider for instance the varied facial expressions of the youths (ill. pp.94–5) over *Persian Sibyl*. The face of the *ignudo* on the right, represented in half-profile, is bathed in a turbulent chiaroscuro; he is looking anxiously over his shoulder toward the viewer, while the companion to his left turns his quiet, sensuous-looking countenance toward him. The figure of the right *ignudo* is reminiscent of the famous *Laocoön Group* (ill. p.48) in its dramatic intensity: This is expressed in the forward-curling hair, the opposed diagonals of torso and limbs, the way the body presses forcefully backward, and not least in the powerful facial expressions.

The large corner-pendentive scene with *Brazen Serpent* (ill. p.110) next to *Prophet Jonah* (ill. pp.118–119) is also an outstanding example of the depiction of the human body in motion—Vasari considered them "even more beautiful and inspired" than all the other corner pictures (Vasari). The extremely vivacious coloring is determined by a triad of yellow, orange, and green tones. The scene shows the terrible punishment of the Israelites who rebelled against God and Moses. On the right are the writhing bodies of the Israelites poisoned by the snakes of Moses; on the left can be seen the survivors who as they flee are raising their arms toward the brazen snake, raised on a staff, who is promising a cure. The bodies of the group on the right, intertwined in a tangle of the most varied movements, are represented with a masterly perspectival foreshortening. On their faces are shown fear, pain, and torment. Vasari described them as the "beautifully

The Flood, 1508–09.
Fresco, 110¼ x 224½ in. (280 x 570 cm).
Vatican, Sistine Chapel, Rome.

There are many discernible cracks in the fresco of *The Flood*, as well as the severe damage caused to the painting by a gunpowder explosion in the Borgo Sant'Angelo in 1797, which broke off large areas of the plaster. The lightning bolt that originally illustrated God's anger—the "wrath of God…pouring down upon them with water, with thunder, and with

lightning" that turns on the people—is no longer discernible (Condivi). The weaknesses in the technical execution of some of the individual figures, especially those on the rocky island, have led scholars to conclude that these must have been carried out by Michelangelo's assistants, using the cartoon he prepared.

SALMON
BOOZ
OBETH

IESSE
DAVID
SALOMON

Josias and his Parents, 1509,
severy over lunette with *Josias, Jechoniah, and Shealtiel (Salathiel)*.
Fresco, 96½ x 133¾ in. (245 x 340 cm).
Vatican, Sistine Chapel, Rome.

The severy is thought to depict the family of Jechoniah with her son
Shealtiel. Characteristic here, as in the other severies and lunettes in
which Michelangelo portrayed Christ's ancestors, is the warmth of
the family scenes: The woman represented in profile is pressing the
child to herself in a loving embrace.

The scene is characterized by the balance of tension in the coloring:
The colored garments of the figures—the pale violet of the woman's
garments and the strong yellow of the shirt worn by the man—stand
out in a lively contrast from the dark background.

◁ Lunettes with *Christ's Ancestors Salmon,
Boaz, and Obed*, 1511–12.
Fresco, 84¾ x 169¼ in. (215 x 430 cm).
Vatican, Sistine Chapel, Rome.

Jesse, David, and Solomon, 1511–12.
Fresco, 84¾ x 169¼ in. (215 x 430 cm).
Vatican, Sistine Chapel, Rome.

Brazen Serpent, 1511, corner pendentive with scenes from the history of the Israelites.
Fresco, 230¼ x 387¾ in. (585 x 985 cm).
Vatican, Sistine Chapel, Rome.

▷ *David and Goliath*, 1509, corner pendentive with scenes from the history of the Israelites.
Fresco, 224½ x 382 in. (570 x 970 cm).
Vatican, Sistine Chapel, Rome.

executed heads shown shrieking and thrown back in despair" (Vasari).

Michelangelo's increasingly adept deployment of colors and the innovations in coloring can be seen to best effect in the figures of the prophets and sibyls. New above all is the use of different, often complementary, colors. In the garments of the prophet *Zechariah* (ill. p.114), for example, the powerful yellow-orange of the tunic forms a lively contrast to the green of the upper garments, which are given great plasticity by the areas of shadow and arrangement of the folds. The beauty and richness of the coloring, combining powerful radiant colors and gentle color shifts, is also shown impressively in the youthful figures of *Delphica* (ill. p.115) and *Libyan Sibyl* (ill. p.4).

Thus, in *Delphica* the cold blue of the coat and the powerful green, red, and orange tones of the lower garments and cape alternate with gentle color shifts; in *Libyan Sibyl* again the strong yellow of the dress that is open at the side and edged

with a silver-gray trim forms a lively contrast to the pale violet tones of the lower garments, which are repeated in her headband. Through the most recent restoration of the frescoes, the luminosity of the colors that Michelangelo sought through the use of pure color pigments, which were hidden under the distemper overpaintings and the layers of dust and rust, and the subtle color shifts were brought out again. With the palette of colors that is manifested in this way, the Sistine ceiling presents itself to the viewer as a work in the tradition of Florentine painting culture.

The highly varied gestural language of the sibyls and prophets in the spandrels was described by the art historian James Beck as a "handbook for this aspect of communication" (Beck). A vivid example of this is the contrasting representation of the prophets *Jeremiah* (ill. p.113) and *Jonah* (ill. pp.118–119). Whereas all the other prophets are shown buried in scripts or holding a scroll, they are seeking the divine vision in another

form. Jeremiah is represented as an old man, with his upper body leaning forward, supporting his chin in his right hand. The prophet appears entirely turned inward, sunken in grief that his prophecies of the fall of Jerusalem have come to pass—he seems to be looking at the divine in his inner world. In contrast, however, the powerful figure of *Jonah*, which Condivi praised as "a stupendous work," is portrayed in a central position over the altar wall, with wonderful perspectival foreshortening (Condivi). Next to *Jonah* is represented the whale in whose belly the prophet remained for three days and nights before being spat out according to the biblical account. Jonah, who is represented leaning backward in a dynamic turning movement of his youthful male body, seems to be eagerly soaking in the light and air that he has regained. He is the only one of the prophets whose face is upturned toward God, who is separating the light from the darkness. Unlike Jeremiah, Jonah is seeking the divine not by looking within, but by looking in the outside world. The expertly formed incursion of light, which immerses his lively, ocher and pink-colored flesh tones in a bright reflection, creates the impression that Jonah is bathing in the glistening light, as

if he were literally sucking the light and air into himself; he seems to be seeing the divine in the external world.

A similar duality can be recognized in the figures of *Persian Sibyl* (ill. p.121) in the figure of an old woman, and the youthful *Delphic Sibyl* (ill. p.115) in her austere beauty. In the age of the Renaissance, the sibyls were shown special reverence, and their prophecies were interpreted as the announcement of Christ's coming. *Persian Sybil*, who is turned away from the viewer looking into a book, is seeking divine wisdom in the ancient Persian scripts. In contrast to the *Persica*, *Delphic Sibyl* is not looking into a book turned away from the world but, holding a scroll in the hand of her horizontally outstretched left arm, she is looking with wide open eyes into the world created by God. Condivi reports that during the works on the painting of the second section of the vault Michelangelo was feeling the full force of the pope's pressure to complete the frescoes, and therefore did not complete them exactly as he had originally intended.

During a visit Julius II made to the scaffold, he is supposed even to have threatened to throw Michelangelo down from the

Prophet Jeremiah and the corner pendentive with the *Punishment of Haman*, 1511, before the restoration. Fresco, 230¼ x 387¾ in. (585 x 985 cm) (spandrel). Vatican, Sistine Chapel, Rome.

▷ *Prophet Jeremiah*, 1511, after the restoration. Fresco, 153½ x 149½ in. (390 x 380 cm). Vatican, Sistine Chapel, Rome.

scaffold, when the artist answered his question as to when he would finish the chapel by saying, "When I can." The official inauguration of the frescoes followed on October 31, 1512, All Saints' Day, with a lavish ceremony that culminated in the pope entering the chapel accompanied by the cardinals in a formal procession. Michelangelo's fame spread rapidly throughout the world. From his fellow artists, including Raphael, Jacopo Pontormo, Rosso Fiorentino, and Domenico Beccafumi, the frescoes of the Sistine ceiling received unanimous admiration and approval.

Vasari's words are representative of the feelings of contemporaries toward Michelangelo's awesome achievement: "The ceiling has proved a veritable beacon to our art, of inestimable benefit to all painters, restoring light to a world that for centuries had been plunged into darkness. Indeed, painters no longer need to seek new inventions, novel attitudes, clothed figures, fresh ways of expression, different arrangements, or sublime subjects, for this work contains every perfection possible under those headings." As a sculptor, Michelangelo had already set standards; now in the ceiling frescoes of the Sistine Chapel he also triumphed as a painter.

HIEREMIAS

ZACHERIAS

DELPHICA

Prophet Ezekiel, 1510, before the restoration.
Fresco, 149½ x 139¾ in. (380 x 355 cm).
Vatican, Sistine Chapel, Rome.

◁ *Study for a prophet*, ca. 1509(?).
Pen and sepia Indian ink, 15½ x 10¼ in. (39 x 26 cm).
Musée Condé, Chantilly, France.

▷ *Prophet Ezekiel*, 1510, after the restoration.

PAGE 114
Prophet Zechariah, 1509.
Fresco, 153½ x 141¾ in. (390 x 360 cm).
Vatican, Sistine Chapel, Rome.

PAGE 115
Delphic Sibyl, ca. 1509.
Fresco, 149½ x 137¾ in. (380 x 350 cm).
Vatican, Sistine Chapel, Rome.

"In *Delphic Sibyl* is concealed Michelangelo's feminine ideal. This woman
stands not below the man but next to him and experiences spirituality not
rationally but intuitively—with wide open eyes" (Stützer).

Head study for *Prophet Jonah*, ca. 1511.
Red chalk, 7¾ x 6¾ in. (19.9 x 17.2 cm).
Casa Buonarroti, Florence.

◁ *Prophet Jonah*, 1511.
Fresco, 157½ x 149½ in. (400 x 380 cm).
Vatican, Sistine Chapel, Rome.

"Then who is not filled with admiration and amazement at the awesome
sight of Jonah, the last figure in the chapel? The vaulting naturally springs
forward, following the curve of the masonry; but through the force of the
art it is apparently straightened out by the figure of Jonah, which bends
in the opposite direction; and thus vanquished by the art of design, with
its lights and shades, the ceiling even appears to recede" (Vasari).

PAGE 120
Prophet Isaiah, 1509.
Fresco, 149½ x 143¾ in. (380 x 365 cm).
Vatican, Sistine Chapel, Rome.

PAGE 121
Persian Sibyl, 1511.
Fresco, 157½ x 149½ in. (400 x 380 cm).
Vatican, Sistine Chapel, Rome.

THE RESTORATION OF THE VAULT FRESCOES IN THE SISTINE CHAPEL

The restoration works on the ceiling frescoes in the 1980s were accompanied by fierce criticism in the art world. Many artists and scientists raised their voices, including Andy Warhol, who, shortly before his death in 1987, together with some other prominent artists such as Louise Bourgeois and Robert Rauschenberg, even sent a petition to Pope John Paul II, asking for the measures to be reconsidered. The newspaper and magazine headlines reflected the fierce controversy that culminated in the sloganeering concept of "Benetton-Michelangelo," with which art criticism at that time attacked the entire restoration as a project that had some questionable aspects.

Eleazar and Matthan, 1511–12, lunette before the restoration.
Fresco, 84¾ x 169¼ in. (215 x 430 cm). Vatican, Sistine Chapel, Rome.

Having begun in June 1980 with the trial cleaning of the *Eleazar and Matthan* lunette (ill. pp.122, 123), which was obscured by layers of candle soot, incense haze, and dust deposited over five centuries, as well as layers of varnish and glue from previous restorations, a committee decided, following the completion of these works in January 1981, to undertake the restoration of all the vault frescoes—a project that was estimated would take twelve years, including the cleaning of *The Last Judgment* on the altar wall. The cleaning works were documented throughout this period by the Nippon Television Network, based in Tokyo, which recorded progress on 147,638 feet (45,000 meters) of 15-mm and 16-mm film.

For the cleaning of the frescoes, the decision had been made to employ a method that used what was known as AB57, a combination solvent. This substance is composed of ammonium bicarbonate, double acid sodium bicarbonate, and a fungicide, as well as carboxymethylcellulose. With the vault frescoes, this combination solvent was left to take effect through paper compresses for approximately three minutes on

the surfaces to be cleaned and was then removed with a natural sponge soaked in distilled water; according to the amount of dirt, this procedure was repeated after twenty-four hours. The water-sensitive parts that had been painted *a secco* were cleaned with special organic solvents or, according to the specification, with a paraloid B72 solution, an acrylic-resin solution, with a water-based solvent. The cleaning process gradually brought out the original radiance of the original colors.

To its critics, the results seemed even during the cleaning works to be almost a desecration of the frescoes; terms like "sacrilege" and "restoration-racket" flew around. While Michelangelo's frescoes had previously given rise to an aura of dark gloom that led the great Michelangelo scholar Charles de Tolnay to refer to the "sphere of shadow and death," (1945) this was now being destroyed; this Michelangelo being exposed under the covering layers that had been thought to be the true Michelangelo was one that people did not want to accept, as Antonio Paolucci explained in connection with the restoration of *David* in 2004. Paolucci saw the criticism as originating from that image—deeply anchored in the collective consciousness— of the smoke-veiled, dramatic chiaroscuro Michelangelo, who could not have worked with this "unrealistic" Mannerist color palette! The Michelangelo that had been brought to light did not accord with the familiar Michelangelo—the emotional and intellectual patina of the centuries was suddenly erased: The true Michelangelo disappointed us because he looked different from the "untrue" one that we all seemed to know and, above all, want to know in that form.

The storm of indignation that was unleashed on the restorers made even famous art critics such as Alexander Eliot compare cleaned details such as *Delphic Sibyl* to "a kind of frightened rubber doll." On the other hand, there were also scientists whose voices may have been drowned out by the criticism from many sides but already at that time were convinced that the restorers were taking the very greatest care and put forward the view that not one of Michelangelo's original brushstrokes

Eleazar and Matthan, 1511–12, lunette after the restoration.
Fresco, 84¾ x 169¼ in. (215 x 430 cm).
Vatican, Sistine Chapel, Rome.

was being lost—as Konrad Oberhuber, then Director of the Albertina Graphische Sammlung in Vienna suggested in 1987.

The care taken by the restorers at the time is proved for instance by the fact that they worked conservatively and gently *ad acquerello*, using watercolors on the parts of the painting severely damaged by cracks; the brushstrokes were introduced in crosshatch and vertically so that these restored areas would remain recognizable to future generations, and it would be visible where the work of Michelangelo's hand ended. The restorers worked while standing on a mobile work platform that was designed based on the plans for Michelangelo's model.

During the cleaning works under the direction of the head conservator of the Vatican Museums, Gianluigi Colalucci, high-tech equipment was also deployed; a computer stored the data from digital photos of the vault in a data bank and in total around 15,000 black-and-white and color photos were taken to record the progress of the cleaning. In addition, there followed various further examinations, including ultraviolet and infrared photographs, as well as microscopic and microbiological analyses. The restoration measures brought many insights into Michelangelo's working technique. For example, it transpired that the vault frescoes were

predominantly executed in *buon fresco* technique and the darker parts had not been painted *a secco*, as the opponents of the restoration had supposed. Instead, the darker color tones proved to be the results of the encrustations of dirt and early, inexpertly executed restoration measures. One aspect on which the specialist world remains divided is the question of how far Michelangelo himself planned *a secco* reworkings, for example on the lapis lazuli blue sky.

The works that concluded in December 1989 also brought insights into the collaboration with his assistants, so that we know today that Michelangelo was not the tormented solitary genius that he describes himself as being in his now-famous sonnet (ill. p.89), but instead was the head of a team of collaborators. Here, too, the image that had generally prevailed of the Sistine Chapel as the work of a single human being was contradicted by the somber reality.

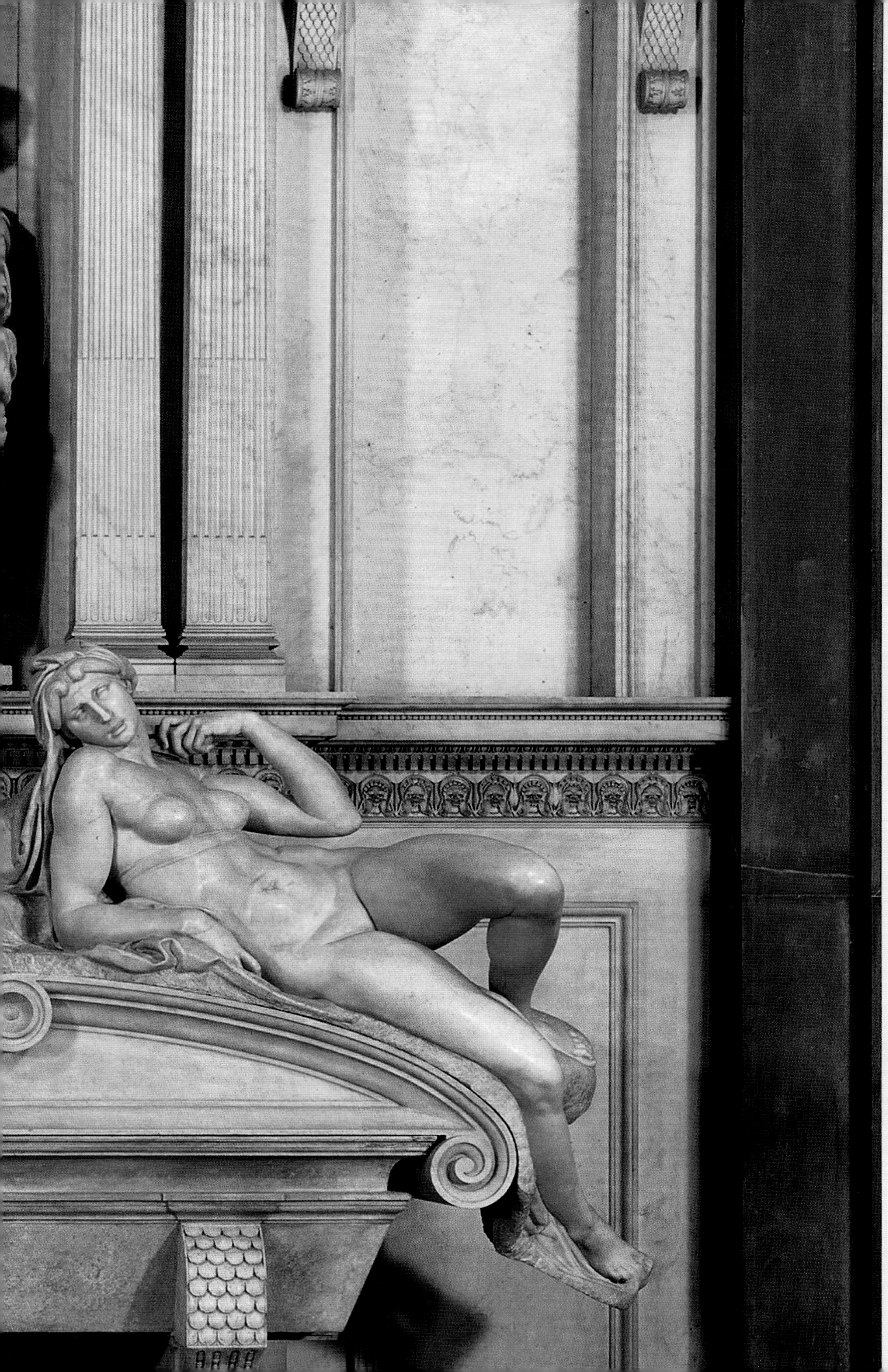

VI. IN THE SERVICE OF THE MEDICI

IN THE SERVICE OF THE MEDICI

THE MEDICI TOMBS IN SAN LORENZO

In a letter of June 17, 1526, that he sent from Florence to his friend Giovan Francesco Fattucci in Rome, Michelangelo reports on the progress of works on the tombs for Giuliano and Lorenzo de' Medici in the New Sacristy in the right wing of the transept of San Lorenzo, which was to be turned into the funeral chapel of the Medici. Between November 1520 and January 1521, he had already worked on the sketches for the creation of the Medici tombs in the New Sacristy (ill. pp.126, 127), for which the shell construction had been completed as far as the cupola and the lantern.

He had received the commission for this from Pope Leo X, Julius II's successor. With Leo X, a member of the House of Medici sat on the papal throne: Giovanni de' Medici, the second eldest son of Lorenzo the Magnificent, had taken over the papal office in March 1513 under the name of Leo X. The election of Giovanni de' Medici as Pope was an important milestone in the resurgence of the House, the Medici having already managed to reinstate their rule over Florence in September 1512. The death of Lorenzo de' Medici, Duke

Studies for the Medici wall tombs (detail of one of the sarcophagi), ca. 1520–21.
Black chalk, 4¼ x 6¼ in. (10.5 x 15.6 cm). Casa Buonarroti, Florence.

PAGES 124–5
Tomb of Lorenzo de' Medici (detail with allegorical studies of *Dusk* and *Dawn*), 1524–31. Marble. San Lorenzo, Medici Chapel, Florence.

"Messer Giovan Francesco,
This coming week I shall have the
figures that are blocked out in the
Sacristy [of San Lorenzo] covered up,
because I want to leave the Sacristy free
for the scarpellini working on the marbles....
And while they are building it in
I thought the vault might be done
and supposed that, with enough men,
it could be done in two or three months....
As to the recess, four columns have been
built in this week—one of them [the fifth]
was built in before.... I'm working as hard
as I can, and in a fortnight's time
I shall get the other 'Captain' [the statue
of Lorenzo, Duke of Urbino] started;
then of the important things, I shall
have only the four 'Rivers' left.
The four figures on the coffers
[i.e., the four times of the day],
the four figures on the ground, which
are the 'Rivers,' the two 'Captains'
[Giuliano and Lorenzo], and 'Our Lady,'
which is going into the Tomb at the top
end [sepultura di testa], are the figures
I want to do myself."

Michelangelo to Giovan Francesco Fattucci,
June 17, 1526.

▷ Studies for the Medici wall tombs, ca. 1520–21.
Black chalk, 10¼ x 7½ in. (26.2 x 18.8 cm). British Museum, London.

of Urbino, in April 1519 had given Leo X and his cousin Cardinal Giulio de' Medici the impetus to make the New Sacristy in San Lorenzo the family's burial place. Next to the duke of Urbino, Lorenzo the Magnificent (born 1492), his brother Giuliano, who was murdered in the Pazzi conspiracy in 1478, and Leo X's brother Giuliano, the duke of Nemours (died 1516), were to find their final resting places. The funeral chapel would serve to glorify the memory of the Medici and thus at the same time demonstrate their claim to grandeur.

The church of San Lorenzo, the family church of the Medici in Florence, was already associated for Michelangelo with one of his most crushing artistic defeats. In 1516, Leo X had announced a competition for the design of the façade of the church that had been constructed by the Florentine Filippo Brunelleschi (1377–1446) (ill. p.130). In May 1518, Michelangelo signed the contract for the façade project, which was to be completed within eight years. In Florence, Michelangelo prepared countless preliminary sketches for the project (ill. pp.130, 131) that he wanted to develop as "both architecturally and sculpturally, the mirror of all Italy." This, however, turned into an utter tragedy. The marble blocks for the façade that were broken in the mainly unexploited quarries of Seravezza near Pietrasanta were smashed during the difficult transportation from the almost impassable terrain. It proved impossible to transport the 3¼-feet (1-meter) high columns, the most important components of the planned façade, from the quarries undamaged. Michelangelo was in complete despair

Jacopo Chimenti da Empoli, *Michelangelo Presents his Model of San Lorenzo to Leo X*, 1617–19. Oil on canvas, 93 x 55½ in. (236 x 141 cm). Casa Buonarroti, Florence.

PAGES 128–9
Tomb of Lorenzo de' Medici, 1524–31, total view.

Tomb of Giuliano de' Medici, 1525–34, total view.
San Lorenzo, Medici Chapel, Florence.

▷ Preliminary sketch for façade of San Lorenzo, ca. 1517–18.
Pen, black chalk, and red chalk, 8¼ x 5¾ in. (21.2 x 14.3 cm).
Casa Buonarroti, Florence.

Sketches of marble blocks for the façade of San Lorenzo, ca. 1516–20.
Pen, folio with fold, folio size each 12½ x 8¾ in. (31.8 x 22 cm).
Archivio Buonarroti, Florence.

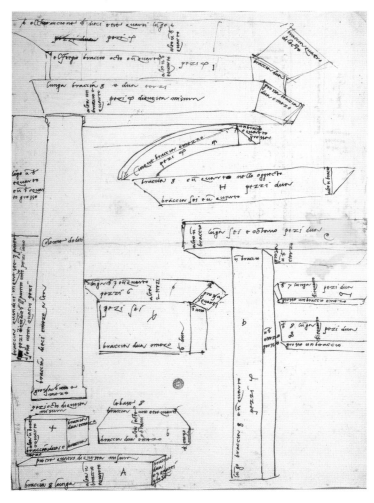

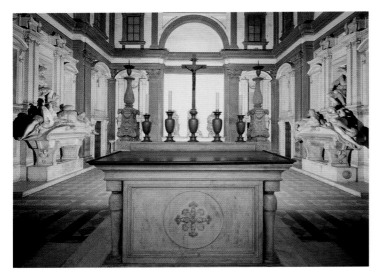

San Lorenzo, New Sacristy, interior view of Medici Chapel with ducal graves and altar.

and suffered acute states of exhaustion. In 1520, Pope Leo X took the commission away from him. Michelangelo had wasted three working years full of trials and tribulations on the façade project for San Lorenzo; it was never executed, and a wooden model now stands in the Casa Buonarroti in Florence.

Leo X died on December 1, 1521. He was succeeded in 1523, after Adrian VI's pontificate lasting just one year, by another pope from the House of Medici: Cardinal Giulio de' Medici, Leo X's cousin, took the Holy Chair as Clement VII. Clement not only became an important patron of Michelangelo; he also ensured the artist's safety in the political turmoil of the period that followed. Furthermore, Clement managed through his mediation in the quarrel between Michelangelo and the Della Rovere heirs about the Julius tomb to bring about a version of the contract that then formed the basis for the tomb's final completion at no financial detriment to Michelangelo. Clement was not only concerned with the progress of works on the Medici tombs in San Lorenzo; in December 1523, he also commissioned Michelangelo to build the library of San Lorenzo, the Laurentian Library, which was to house the valuable collection of books and manuscripts that had been assembled by Lorenzo the Magnificent.

In the creation of the Medici Chapel (ill. pp.132, 133), and even more so in the Laurentian Library (ill. p.146), Michelangelo forged a new architectural language that broke with the prevailing classical canon of forms of the Renaissance, largely based on Vitruvius, and thus paved the way for Mannerism in architecture.

PAGES 134–5
Tomb of Lorenzo de' Medici (detail of seated figure Lorenzo), 1524–31. Marble, 70 in. (178 cm) high. San Lorenzo, Medici Chapel, Florence.

Tomb of Giuliano de' Medici (detail of seated figure Guiliano), 1525–34. Marble, 70 in. (178 cm) high. San Lorenzo, Medici Chapel, Florence.

The "ornamentation in a composite order" with which Michelangelo breaks through the established conventions of ornamentation is the expression of an individual language of forms in which individual architectural elements are newly assembled with artistic freedom (Vasari). This is shown very vividly in the design of the walls: They are divided by the interplay between white marble and darker *pietra serena*, the gray sandstone typical of the Florentine region, which was used for the pilasters, capitals, cornices, archivolts, window frames, and triangular gables. They no longer have a static function as in the classical Renaissance canon; instead they become sculpturally conceived, independent architectural elements that lead to a new form of expressive tension in their overall effect in the spatial structure of the chapel.

Interior view of the cupola in San Lorenzo, New Sacristy, Medici Chapel, Florence.

Interior view of Medici Chapel with the tomb of Giuliano de' Medici and *Medici Madonna*, flanked by the patron saints of the Medici, *Cosmas* and *Damian*. The latter were executed by Michelangelo's collaborators Raffaello da Montelupo—from his model and Giovanni Angelo da Montorsoli.

In his conception of the tombs, Michelangelo had originally envisaged, as with the Julius tomb, a free-standing monument that would accommodate all the graves together. He then retreated from this idea and finally adopted the solution of placing the ducal graves at the side walls of the chapel, while a double grave on the entrance wall would take the sarcophagi of Lorenzo the Magnificent and his brother Giuliano, as well as the statue of the Madonna, flanked by the family saints Cosmas and Damian. The double grave was not executed, but the statues of the Madonna, the so-called *Medici Madonna* (ill. p.142), and the saints were. In creating the seated figures of the dukes, Michelangelo drew on the antique vocabulary of forms (ill. pp.134, 135). Both dukes are represented in the style of dynastic glorification with Roman breastplates. Lorenzo

is on his throne, with a deeply pensive expression, while Giuliano has an open gaze, his upper body turned to one side; their gestures and facial expressions give them the demeanor of Roman imperators. The aloofness radiated by the figures is far removed from the actual characters of those portrayed. Giuliano, who was born in 1479, the youngest son of Lorenzo the Magnificent and the brother of Pope Leo X, who returned to Florence in 1512 after an eighteen-year exile, was known for his gloomy temperament and had furthermore become bedridden through a tuberculosis infection. Lorenzo, born in 1492, Giuliano's nephew, is described as cunning and cowardly, especially in his battle with the Della Rovere for the dukedom of Urbino; similarly his behavior was said to be arrogant and his lifestyle hedonistic. He fell ill with syphilis, which had spread

rapidly throughout Italy following the occupation of Naples (1492–1503) by French troops. The disease first appeared in Florence in 1496, and Lorenzo died "wretchedly of 'the French disease' two decades later" (Beck).

Yet for Michelangelo it was not a matter of individual resemblance: Above and beyond dynastic glorification, the ducal figures become symbols of the *vita activa* in the livelier figure of Giuliano and the *vita contemplativa* in the pensive-looking Lorenzo. Panofsky referred to "two universal types of human existence" whose contrasting nature Michelangelo illustrated in the two figures, recognizing in them "the eternal antithesis between the active and the contemplative, the Jovian and the Saturnine, ways of life—both roads to immortality—which was one of the leitmotifs of Neoplatonic thought" (Panofsky).

On each of the vaulted sarcophagi under the seated figures of the dukes rest a male and a female figure—the personifications

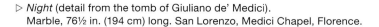

Day (detail from the tomb of Giuliano de' Medici).
Marble, 72¾ in. (185 cm) long. San Lorenzo, Medici Chapel, Florence.

▷ *Night* (detail from the tomb of Giuliano de' Medici).
Marble, 76½ in. (194 cm) long. San Lorenzo, Medici Chapel, Florence.

of day and night, assigned to Giuliano de' Medici (ill. pp.136, 137), and dawn and dusk (ill. p.138) to Lorenzo. Michelangelo provided them with the corresponding attributes, thus the female figure of *Night* with the owl and the bundle of opium poppy heads on which her left foot is resting. *The Times of Day* are allegories of the passage of time to which the human being is subject.

The allegories are distinguished by a powerful musculature that is especially impressive to observe on the figure of *Night*, for example in the powerful, bent thigh and also in the back musculature of *Day*. Michelangelo's preparatory studies attest once more his intensive preoccupation with anatomy, which did not hinder him from exercising a certain freedom in portraying proportions, if we consider, for example, the extremely elongated ribcage of *Night*. The figures rest, the upper bodies captured in a turning motion with their imposing limbs on the vaulted sarcophagus lids; the legs extending far into the space and hanging downward evoke an upward movement in the bodies, as well as the impression of floating in the space. The facial expressions of the figures are striking in their restrained melancholy; they seem to betray an insurmountable sense of defeat—a melancholy that also appears in the countenance of *Medici Madonna*, which is placed on the wall opposite the altar (ill. p.142) and is spatially

Dawn (detail from the tomb of Lorenzo de' Medici).
Marble, 81 in. (206 cm) long.
San Lorenzo, Medici Chapel, Florence.

◁ *Dusk* (detail from the tomb of Lorenzo de' Medici).
Marble, 76¾ in. (195 cm) long.
San Lorenzo, Medici Chapel, Florence.

▷ *Dawn* (detail of upper body).

"Day and Night speak, in these words:
'We with our swift course have led Duke
Giuliano to death; it is only right that he
should gain revenge on us, as he does.
And his revenge is this: that since we have
killed him, he being killed has deprived
us of light, and by closing his eyes has
shut ours, which no longer shed light on
the earth. What, then, might he not have
done for us if he had lived?'"

Michelangelo on his figures
in the Medici Chapel.

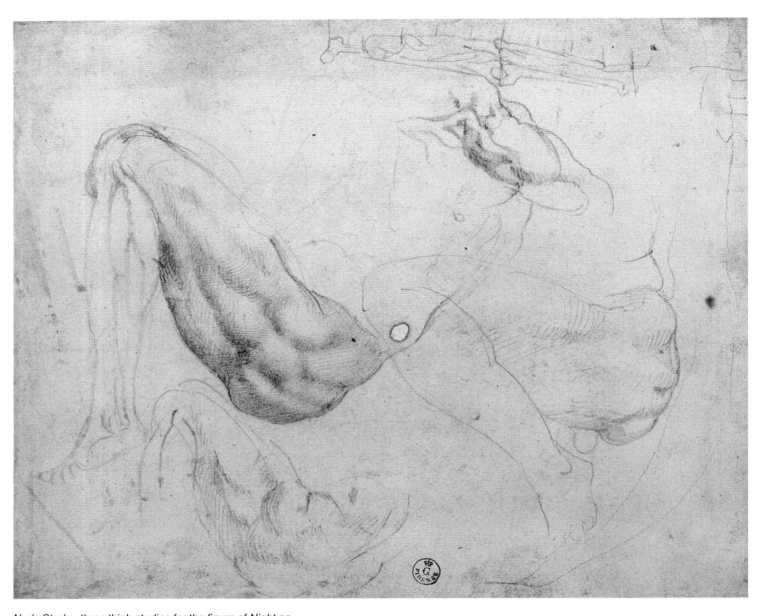

Nude Study—three thigh studies for the figure of *Night* on
the tomb of Giuliano de' Medici, ca. 1525–31. Black chalk,
13½ x 11 in. (34.5 x 28 cm). Gabinetto dei Disegni e delle
Stampe degli Uffizi, Florence.

The female allegorical figures are impressive in their mighty,
extremely powerful limbs, which seem rather to belong to male
bodies. Michelangelo did not in fact draw his female nudes from
nature, but used male models for them.

▷ *Day*, view of back, detail from the tomb for Giuliano de' Medici.

▷ Studies for the back and the left arm of the recumbent figure of *Day*,
ca. 1524. Black chalk, 7¾ x 10 in. (19.6 x 25.7 cm).
Teylers Museum, Haarlem, Netherlands.

This impressive study demonstrates Michelangelo's masterly portrayal of
the anatomy of the body in motion. The varied modeling with chiaroscuro
and the fine internal drawing make the muscles of the back and arm of
the upper body, captured in a turning motion, emerge plastically, almost
springing forward. The force of the bodily tension can literally be sensed.
The art historian Wolfgang Braunfels writes here trenchantly: "There
are two basic motifs that concerned Michelangelo and him alone: the
wrestling upward of the body out of the stone that holds it bound, and
the threat posed by a drop in the gravity of one's own body, which the
power of the mind is seeking to overcome" (Braunfels).

140

Study for *Madonna and Child*, ca. 1520.
Black chalk, red chalk, heightened with white,
Indian ink, 21¼ x 15½ in. (54.1 x 39.6 cm).
Casa Buonarroti, Florence.

◁ *Madonna and Child (Medici Madonna)*, begun 1521.
Marble, 89 in. (226 cm) high (including plinth).
San Lorenzo, Medici Chapel, Florence.

▷ *Night* (detail from the tomb of Giuliano de' Medici).
Marble. San Lorenzo, Medici Chapel, Florence.

connected with the seated figures of the dukes by the way in
which they are turned toward it.

In the *Madonna*, Michelangelo takes up the type of the
breast-feeding Virgin Mary, the *Madonna lactans*: The Christ
child on her lap turns in a violent twisting motion toward the
mother's breast. The body line of the *Madonna* is reminiscent
of the dynamic curvature of the figure of *Victor* (ill. p.77),
which Michelangelo is thought to have created during this

period for the Julius tomb. The melancholy in the countenances
of Mary and the figures of *The Times of Day* has been interpreted
by Antonio Forcellino as an expression of the approximately
fifty-year-old Michelangelo's own sense of defeat and
exhaustion; the author sees Mary's pain as reflecting the
suffering of the artist recognizing defeat, enslaved with
no prospect of release. The creation of the Medici Chapel
(ill. pp.132, 133) remained altogether fragmentary when
Michelangelo left Florence in 1534. He had designed further
elements for the ornamentation of the ducal graves, including
frescoes in the lunettes over the graves, a lavish plastic
decoration on the architrave, allegorical statues in the niches
on either side of the seated figures, and four further studies of
river gods underneath the sarcophagi.

Study with grotesque heads and sketch of a group of wrestlers,
ca. 1525–30(?). Red chalk, black chalk (in parts),
10 x 13¾ in. (25.5 x 35 cm). British Museum, London.

The artistic freedom in the painting of the Medici Chapel is
reflected in the grotesque ornamentation that adorns the walls
and the decorative sculpture.

THE LAURENTIAN LIBRARY

Michelangelo's confident departure from the classical
architectural canon of the Renaissance goes one stage further
in the construction of the Laurentian Library, which he built
on to San Lorenzo. After the first designs that he made in 1524,
the work was brought to a standstill by the political upheaval
that culminated in the Sack of Rome in 1527 when Charles V's
troops plundered the city. It was not until 1530, after the end
of the Florentine republic and the return of the Medici, that
Michelangelo resumed the work.

There were two major construction phases: the reading room
constructed in 1524–27 and the vestibule with the monumental
staircase that originated in 1530–34. The reading room

◁ Candelabrum base with grotesque decoration (from Michelangelo's
designs). San Lorenzo, Medici Chapel, Florence.

(ill. p.146), whose side walls are divided by pilasters, is impressive
primarily for its wood carvings, such as in the lavishly coffered
ceiling or the carving on the reading desks; these were carried
out according to Michelangelo's designs by his collaborators.

The contrast between the long, extended reading room
leading into spatial depth and the deeper-set vestibule rising
into the vertical line can be interpreted as a deliberate violation
of the classical canon, which continues in the individual
architectural elements (ill. p.147). This becomes especially clear
in the structure of the wall: Between the projecting wall surfaces
are set double columns that no longer have a load-bearing
function, any more than do the volute-brackets underneath
them. The architectural elements stand alone; freed from any
tectonic connection with a spatial structure and no longer
conceived as an organic whole, they function as autonomous
sculptural decorative elements. Vasari described in detail the
"audacity" of Michelangelo's architectural language and the

Laurentian Library, large reading room with coffered ceilings and reading desks from Michelangelo's designs of 1534. San Lorenzo, Laurentian Library, Florence.

▷ Laurentian Library, vestibule (Ricetto) with staircase leading to library; shell construction 1524–26, staircase designed by Michelangelo 1534, staircase completed 1559 by Bartolomeo Ammanati, library opened 1571.

Preliminary sketch for a reading desk for the Laurentian Library, 1524–33. Pen and red chalk, 6¼ x 7¾ in. (15.8 x 19.9 cm). Casa Buonarroti, Florence.

emancipation from "the bonds and chains" of the canon of classical rules in the architecture of the Laurentian Library: "Nor was there ever seen such resolute grace, in both detail and overall effect…nor any stairway more commodious. And in this stairway, he made such strange breaks in the design of the steps, and he departed in so many details and so widely from normal practice, that everyone was astonished" (Vasari).

The substantial staircase was certainly designed by Michelangelo but the extension of the stairwell was interrupted in the 1520s, so the staircase was completed only from 1559 by the Florentine architect Bartolomeo Ammanati (1511–92) based on a clay model of Michelangelo's. Michelangelo sent the clay model of the staircase in January 1559 to Ammanati, not without a few well-meaning pieces of advice concerning its execution: "I've contrived to maintain the same method;

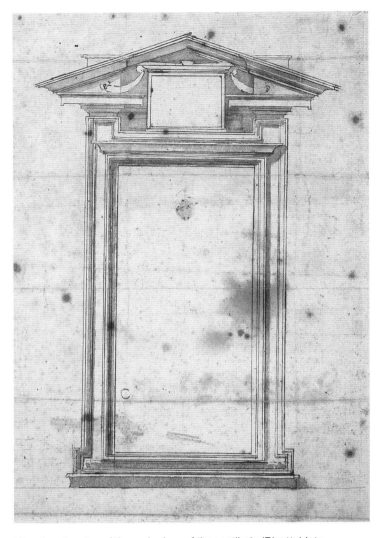

Elevation drawing of the main door of the vestibule (Ricetto) into the reading room of the Laurentian Library, originally planned for a tabernacle of the vestibule, then used for the door, 1526–33.
Pen, with wash, 13½ x 9½ in. (34.6 x 23.9 cm).
Casa Buonarroti, Florence.

Preliminary design for a wall architecture of the Laurentian Library, 1524.
Pen, black chalk, 8¼ x 11½ in. (21 x 29.3 cm).
Casa Buonarroti, Florence.

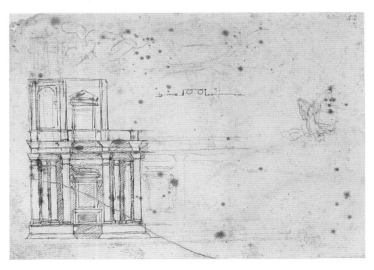

I do not want the side stairs to have balusters at the ends, like the main flight, but a seat between every two steps, as indicated by the embellishments. There is no need for me to tell you anything about bases, fillets for these plinths and other ornaments, because you are resourceful, and being on the spot will see what is needed much better than I can. As to the height and length, take up as little space as you can by narrowing the extremity as you think fit. It is my opinion that if the said staircase were made in wood—that is to say in a fine walnut—it would be better than in stone, and more in keeping with the desks, the ceiling, and the door [of the library]. I think that's all. I'm all yours, old, blind, deaf, and inept in hands and in body." Michelangelo's plan for a wooden staircase was not carried out by Ammanati, who built it in *pietro serena*, the gray sandstone of the Florentine region.

DIFFICULT YEARS IN FLORENCE

The long creative period in Florence from 1518 to 1534 was a very difficult time in Michelangelo's life. It began with the drama of the transportation of the marble blocks from the quarries near Pietrasanta, which was followed by the political upheavals that obstructed the completion of his work. After the Sack of Rome in 1527, the terrible culmination of the enduring power struggle between King Francis I of France and the German Holy Roman Emperor Charles V, which shook the foundations of the Christian world, and during the subsequent dramatic years of the Florentine republic, in fall 1528 Michelangelo took up a post as an advisor in the construction of the fortifications in the service of the republican government. Following the re-expulsion of the Medici from Florence in 1527, this was headed by the *gonfaloniere* Niccolò di Piero Capponi.

In January 1529, Michelangelo became a member of the Defense Council of Nine and in April that year took over the construction supervision of the fortifications of Florence, which was under attack from the emperor's and the pope's troops. In this period, he created many fortification plans for the city gates (ill. p.151) that never actually came to fruition. In September 1529, the fall of the republic seemed to be irreversible, and Michelangelo fled to Venice, but soon returned in November. On August 12, 1530, Florence surrendered and the Medici returned and reestablished their rule. Alessandro de' Medici was appointed by the Spanish as duke in Florence, which was negotiated by Clement VII in Bologna with Charles V, with regard to his family interests.

Michelangelo, who was by then regarded as an enemy and traitor of the Medici, feared for his life; he knew that he was being pursued by the hatred of the Medici duke. He was hunted down, but could not be found. The prior of San Lorenzo granted him protection in San Lorenzo (ill. p.150). Clement VII, himself a Medici, was the person who pardoned him; he

Laurentian Library, vestibule (Ricetto), western wall,
San Lorenzo, Florence.

Front view of the staircase in the vestibule of the Laurentian Library.

wanted Michelangelo to continue attending to the work in San Lorenzo, so Michelangelo resumed the works on the Medici tombs and the Laurentian Library in 1530.

The small, unfinished marble figure of *David-Apollo* (ill. pp.152, 153) that Michelangelo created in this period reflects the merciless precedence of interests: Of all people, it was the pope's emissary Baccio Valori who commissioned Michelangelo to chisel the sculpture for Alessandro de' Medici. Valori was among the most violent persecutors of the Medici enemies, and his helpers had searched for Michelangelo to avenge the humiliation of the Medici.

Michelangelo's health suffered severe collapses in the long years of the Florentine period: While the physical strains he underwent in the quarries of Seravezza had already exhausted him, he also found himself in a poor state of health in 1531

Wall drawing with studies of allegorical figures for the Medici tombs, ca. 1530. Charcoal on plaster.

The drawing was discovered in 1975 in a room behind the Medici Chapel, where Michelangelo is thought to have stayed under the protection of the Prior of San Lorenzo after the Medici's return to Florence.

▷ Fortification study for the Porta a San Miniato, Florence, 1528.
Pen, with wash, 11½ x 16¼ in. (29.1 x 41.2 cm). Casa Buonarroti, Florence.

▷ Fortification study for the Prato d'Ognissanti, 1528.
Pen, with wash, red chalk, 11¼ x 15½ in. (28.3 x 39.6 cm). Casa Buonarroti, Florence.

during the work on the Medici tombs. Yet not only was he troubled by his health in this period; his life was also shaken by some personal blows of fate: In 1528, his favorite brother Buonarroto died of the plague, and early in 1531 he lost his father Ludovico. The artist expressed his pain and grief about these losses in an elegy (see p.154).

In September 1534, Michelangelo finally decided to leave his home city and settle in Rome. The combination of the worries caused him by the Julius tomb and the threats of the Della Rovere heirs, in particular the duke of Urbino, Francesco Maria della Rovere, were still hanging over him, as the letter from Giovanni Battista di Paolo Mini attests. Yet a visit concerning this matter to Pope Clement in Rome early in 1532 brought a ray of light into Michelangelo's life: He met the young Roman nobleman Tommaso de' Cavalieri, with whom he would from then on be bound by a deep affection.

"IF I DIE BY BURNING, I HOPE TO RISE AGAIN"— MICHELANGELO AND TOMMASO DE' CAVALIERI

"Inadvisedly, Messer Tommao, my dearest lord, I was prompted to write to your lordship, not in answer to any letter I had received from you, but being the first to move…. And if, as I've said, I were ever to have the assurance of pleasing your lordship in anything, I would devote to you the present and the time to come that remains to me, and should very deeply regret that I cannot have the past over again, in order to serve you longer than with the future only, which will be short, since I'm so old."

Even this first letter that Michelangelo wrote to Tommaso de' Cavalieri in Rome in the last few days of December 1532 bears open witness to the artist's intense affection for the attractive young Roman nobleman, who was then just

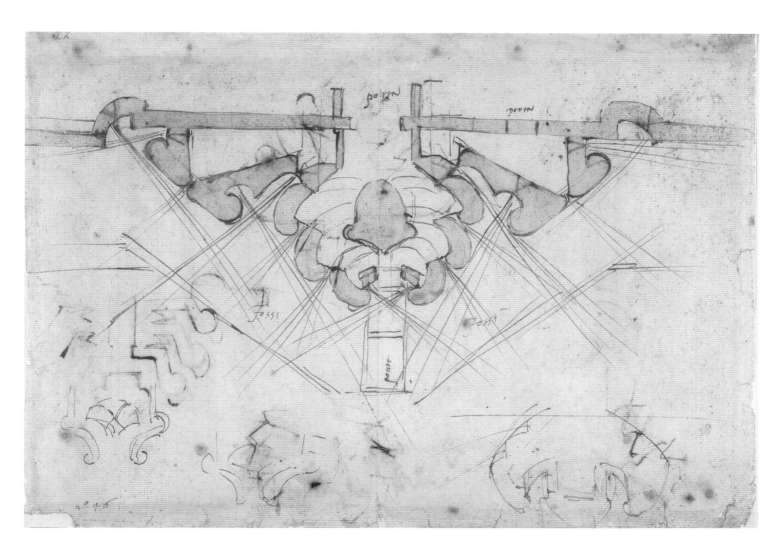

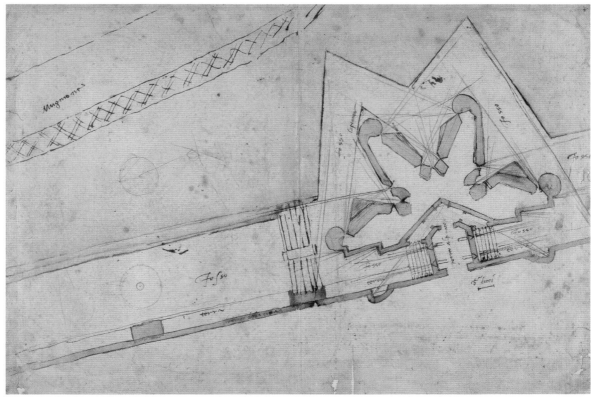

*"With your departure; so I must distinguish
when I weep, write or speak between your son
who died first and you who died later,
of whom I am now speaking.

One was my brother, and you the father of
us both; to him I am bound by love, to you
by obligation; I do not know which affliction
crushes or torments me more.

My memory indeed paints my brother,
but you it sculpts alive within my heart—this
more afflicts my heart and stains my face.

Yet it comforts me that, while my brother
paid time's debt when he was unripe,
you paid it when mature, for if someone dies
when he is old this brings us less pain."*

In these verses, Michelangelo mourns the death of his
father and his brother Buonarroto.

twenty-two years old, nearly forty years younger than Michelangelo. As Vasari reports, Michelangelo had made a portrait of Cavalieri "in a life-size cartoon" (Vasari). The portrait is missing but stylistically it may have resembled the only preserved portrait drawing from Michelangelo's hand, *Portrait of Andrea Quaratesi* (1512–85), who came from a respected Florentine banking family and is thought to have been a drawing student of Michelangelo's (ill. p.155). Michelangelo addressed countless poems and letters to the young Cavalieri and around 1533 he gave him a series of drawings on mythological themes (ill. pp.156, 157) to express his deep affection for the young Roman.

The Michelangelo literature interprets the drawings on the one hand as an expression of Michelangelo's intense erotic desire, and *The Rape of Ganymede* as the illustration of an erotic ecstasy that undoubtedly speaks of the artist's identification with the eagle, who embraces the youth in free flight as in a loving union (Forcellino). Other viewpoints consider them as allegories of a love primarily characterized by Neoplatonic ideas. "But it is almost beyond doubt that Michelangelo intended them as allegories of Platonic love, Ganymede symbolizing divinely

inspired, and Tityus sensual love, and that these symbols adumbrated deep and tragic emotions in his relationship with Cavalieri" (Wittkower).

Michelangelo himself generally maintained silence concerning his sexual life. Yet already his contemporaries nursed the reproach of homosexuality according to the Italian writer Pietro Aretino (1492–1556) in a defamatory letter in November 1545 in which he denounced Michelangelo, the creator of *The Last Judgment*; in it Aretino tried to persuade Michelangelo to give him a drawing by saying "this act of courtesy would silence the envious tongues that say that only certain Gerards and Thomases dispose of them" (Addington Symonds).

To this day, the judgment as to Michelangelo's possible homosexuality is ultimately based on conjecture. It is certain that Michelangelo's friendship with Cavalieri may in no event be prematurely and one-sidedly judged in terms of the contemporary concept of homosexuality. The art historian James H. Beck explained conclusively in his portrayal of "Michelangelo's sexuality" that the claim that Michelangelo

Head of a Young Woman, 1518–20. Red chalk, 8 x 6½ in. (20.5 x 16.5 cm). University of Oxford, Ashmolean Museum, England.

PAGES 152–3
David-Apollo, ca. 1530–32 (begun as David and modified into an Apollo), unfinished. Marble, 57½ in. (146 cm) high (including plinth). Bargello Museum, Florence.

▷ *Portrait of Andrea Quaratesi*, ca. 1532.
Black chalk, 16¼ x 11½ in. (41.1 x 29.2 cm). British Museum, London.

was homosexual lacks any "solid historical support." In support of his thesis, Beck quotes not only Michelangelo's sparse comments on his sexual life—such as his statement about abstinence: "I have always practiced it. If you wish to prolong your life, restrain yourself as much as you can..." but also the examples of Ficino and his Neoplatonic theory of forms, as well as Savonarola's sermons, that promoted sexual continence as an ideal for which it was worth striving. Furthermore, fear of the syphilis that was raging at that time and strict punishments of homosexuality might have acted as incentives for Michelangelo in "his control of sexual appetite" (Beck).

Let us conclude by returning briefly to Wittkower's interpretation of the meaning inherent in the drawings made for Cavalieri. This can be extended to a fundamental characteristic of Michelangelo's creative work. It is the deployment of the traditional language of forms and contents that are transposed and newly infused with individual freedom, whether in the composition of the architecture in the Medici Chapel and the Laurentian Library, or in the "highly charged personal overtones" of the drawings for Cavalieri (Wittkower).

This emancipation from the prevailing rules, this freedom for individuality, gave Michelangelo's art an impact for centuries to come. One work in which this freedom of creative genius can again be seen was undertaken by Michelangelo—albeit reluctantly—after his move to Rome: the monumental fresco of *The Last Judgment*.

"With your beautiful eyes I see a sweet light that with my blind eyes I certainly cannot see; with your feet I carry on my back a weight that my lame feet certainly could not bear.

Though lacking feathers I fly with your wings; with your mind I am always carried to heaven; on your decision turns whether I am pale or red, cold in the sun, warm in the coldest mists.

In your will alone does my will consist, my thoughts spring from your heart, with your breath are my words formed.

On my own I seem like the moon left to itself, for our eyes can see nothing whatever in the heavens except what is lit up by the sun."

Michelangelo's sonnet of 1534 is addressed to Tommaso de' Cavalieri.

The Rape of Ganymede (above), *The Fall of Phaeton* (middle), and *The Transformation of the Heliades*, ca. 1533. Black chalk, 16¼ x 9¼ in. (41.3 x 23.5 cm). Windsor Royal Library, England.

In this connection, the recently discovered document concerning Tommaso de' Cavalieri's drawing collection should be mentioned. This contract dated February 16, 1580, about the sale of his drawing collection lists far fewer drawings by Michelangelo in the Roman nobleman's possession than was previously supposed; in total according to this there were only four drawings by Michelangelo that the Roman nobleman sold (Zöllner et al.). This sensational discovery reignited the debate about the attribution of Michelangelo's drawings, which is one of the most exciting and greatest challenges of Michelangelo research.

Ideal Female Head in Three-Quarter Profile (Cleopatra), ca. 1533–34. Black chalk, 9¼ x 7¼ in. (23.4 x 18.2 cm). Casa Buonarroti, Florence.

The portrait of Cleopatra is one of the famous ideal or "Divine heads"— a name that comes from Vasari—from the series of drawings that Michelangelo gave primarily to his beloved Tommaso de' Cavalieri. The folio with *The Rape of Ganymede* also belongs in this category of gift drawings.

THE GREAT PAINTINGS OF
THE MATURE YEARS

"THE DEAD SEEMED DEAD, THE LIVING SEEMED ALIVE"—*THE LAST JUDGMENT*

On September 25, 1534, Pope Clement VII died, only two days after Michelangelo had left his home city of Florence to settle finally in Rome. Clement had already commissioned

Composition sketch for *The Last Judgment*, ca. 1534. Black chalk, 16½ x 11¾ in. (41.9 x 29.7 cm). Casa Buonarroti, Florence.

PAGES 158–9
The Last Judgment, detail of the middle lower section with the horde of trumpet-blowing angels.
Fresco. Vatican, Sistine Chapel, altar wall, Rome.

Michelangelo in 1533 for the fresco of *The Last Judgment* (ill. p.161), which was to decorate the altar wall of the Sistine Chapel. Paul III, the newly elected pope from the House of Farnese, who assumed his pontificate on October 3, 1534, proved to be firmly resolved to keep Michelangelo in his service and to have the fresco of *The Last Judgment* carried out by him. Michelangelo, however, showed some reluctance, citing his contractual obligation toward the Della Rovere heirs for the completion of the Julius tomb. The pope is then supposed to have furiously threatened Michelangelo with tearing up the contract for the tomb and forcefully demonstrated his resolve that Michelangelo should serve him in every instance.

Despite these initial disputes, the new pope was to become an important patron of Michelangelo, who was almost the same age as him. Following Clement VII's pontificate, Paul III had set himself the task of reviving the Church and along with it restoring the authority of the Papal States. His reform endeavors finally led in 1545 to the Council of Trent, which ushered in the Counter-Reformation. Michelangelo soon enjoyed an extraordinary reputation with Paul III, who on September 1, 1535, by papal decree appointed him to be "Supreme Architect, Sculptor, and Painter to the Apostolic Palace," at an astoundingly high salary of 1200 scudi.

Early in 1535, Michelangelo began work on *The Last Judgment* with the erection of a scaffold. In addition, two windows in the altar wall had to be bricked up and the wall had to be prepared with a brick veneer—this protrudes by about 12 inches (30 centimeters), and is still visible today in the upper region. At the same time, the artist was occupied with the cartoon drawings for the figures that served as models for the fresco painting (ill. p.160). Early that year the colors were also procured, including the valuable and expensive lapis lazuli from the Orient that Michelangelo used to create the enormous sky area in *The Last Judgment*. He received support in his work from his assistant Francesco Urbino, who was primarily responsible for mixing the colors and transferring the cartoon drawings onto the plaster.

The Last Judgment, 1536–41, total view.
Fresco, 55¾ x 43½ ft. (17 x 13.3 m).
Vatican, Sistine Chapel, altar wall, Rome.

The Last Judgment, upper section, before the restoration.
Vatican, Sistine Chapel, altar wall, Rome.

The restoration of *The Last Judgment* immediately followed the vault
frescoes and was finished in March 1994. Because of the easily soluble
pigments of the lapis lazuli blue, the cleaning of the sky zone was
especially difficult. The work was done with natural sponges, which
were soaked first in deionized water and then in ammonium carbonate
and could only be pressed with the greatest care.

▷ The *Last Judgment*, detail of the upper section, Christ as world judge
and his mother Mary, to the left of Christ the elect with John the Baptist,
on the right the group of the elect with Peter, who is passing two keys
to Christ, beneath the figure of Christ St. Lawrence (with gridiron) and
St. Bartholomew (with flayed skin).

Michelangelo's first idea for *The Last Judgment* planned an
integration of the preexisting fresco decoration on the altar wall
of the Sistine Chapel, which included the frescoes with the first
two scenes from the lives of Moses and Christ and Perugino's
altar picture of Mary's assumption into heaven, as well as the
two lunettes depicting Christ's ancestors that Michelangelo had
already carried out. However, he then decided to have these
decorations removed. At the beginning of 1536, the plasterwork
on the altar wall was prepared for the fresco painting. In
December 1540, the works had already progressed so far that
the upper part of the painting could be unveiled. During this an
accident occurred in which Michelangelo fell from the scaffold
in the chapel and injured his leg. The obstinate Michelangelo

only reluctantly allowed himself to be treated but soon made a recovery. Having returned to work, he completed his painting within a few months, so that it was presented to the public on October 31, 1541, All Saints' Eve, as the Sistine ceiling frescoes had been twenty-nine years earlier.

When the painting was unveiled in the presence of many famous contemporaries the viewers were astounded at the awesome creative power, the *terribilità*, of Michelangelo, who had managed to complete this monumental fresco in only six years. On a huge surface of over 2153 square feet (200 square meters), Michelangelo illustrated in his *Last Judgment* nearly four hundred figures, which are grouped around the judging Christ in the center of the painting.

Innovative in the conception was the absence of the architectural frame that is still provided in the illusional architecture of ceiling painting: thus, the chapel seems to open out into the space of the sky; the slightly projecting wall in the upper area reinforces the power of the dramatic vision. In this fusion of iconographic and actual space, Michelangelo prefigures a characteristic feature of Mannerism.

The composition is characterized by the upward and downward movements of the bodies, which are arranged on various levels and in spatial depth. The art historian Loren Partridge has vividly described the structure with the image of a pair of scales: "On a patch of earth and against a deep blue sky are four bands of figures, each tipped toward the right as if they were giant balance beams responding to the ascent of the elect on the left and the descent of the damned on the right" (Partridge).

In the center of the monumental fresco stands Christ, (ill. pp.161, 162–3) portrayed as youthful and clean-shaven, just rising from his throne in the clouds. His right arm is raised "in the manner of a man who wrathfully damns the guilty and banishes them from His presence to eternal fire; and, with His left hand held out toward His right side, it seems as if He is gently gathering the righteous to Him" (Condivi). The holy Virgin on the right of Christ is turning her face, on which can be seen an expression of anxious concern, as a sign of the mercy of the group of those risen from the dead. As in a close-pressed circle, the saints, apostles, elect, and martyrs gather around the central group with Christ and the Virgin Mary. Starting from the left side we can recognize, among others, the following figures: Adam, with shoulders covered in an animal skin—in the Michelangelo literature this figure is also interpreted as John the Baptist—St. Andrew with the Cross, St. Lawrence with the gridiron, and St. Bartholomew, who is holding his flayed skin (ill. pp.166–7), which is generally thought to contain Michelangelo's self-portrait—a reference to the artist's preoccupation with his own death, also connected with the hope of resurrection. Over Bartholomew on the right can be seen St. Peter with the keys (ill. pp.162–3); diagonally behind him is thought to be John the Baptist. On the right below this group are portrayed, from the left: Dismas, the penitent robber, with the Cross, Simon the Zealot with the saw, St. Blasius with the wool-combs, St. Catherine of Alexandria with the broken wheel, St. Sebastian kneeling with the arrows in his hand (ill. pp.166–7), and behind him Simon of Cyrene, who is carrying the Cross.

In the center of the group arranged underneath them are the trumpet-blowing angels (ill. pp.168–9) described by John in Revelation, the only prophetic book of the New Testament (Revelation 8, 9, 11) "who with trumpets at their lips summon the dead to judgment from the four corners of the earth" (Condivi).

▷ *The Last Judgment*, detail of the middle right section with the elect.

The cross-bearing figure on the right margin is interpreted as Simon of Cyrene; underneath this powerful figure appears St. Sebastian with the arrows.

◁ Study for a *Risen Christ*, ca. 1532–34(?). Black chalk, 16¼ x 10¾ in. (41.4 x 27.4 cm). British Museum, London.

▷ *The Last Judgment*, detail of the right zone underneath Christ with the group of saints: (from the left) Simon the Zealot, Dismas (the penitent robber), Blasius, Andrew, Catherine of Alexandria, and Sebastian.

The figures of St. Catherine and St. Blasius were newly frescoed after Michelangelo's death by Daniele da Volterra. Their original postures as well as their nakedness were censured as offensive by the Council of Trent. Daniele also had to paint over many other private body parts; he carried out these "corrections" in tempera painting. Into the flayed skin that illustrates the martyrdom of Bartholomew, Michelangelo painted his self-portrait.

To their left is portrayed the group of those risen from the dead, who are ascending to heaven, and underneath them again the group of those rising from the dead, who are clambering up laboriously from the earth, some of them still in the form of a skeleton. To the right of the angel can be seen the damned falling into hell. In the lowest level of the right picture zone, they are crossing the Acheron in an overloaded boat, steered by the boatswain Charon, who with a wild expression is threatening the damned with the oar (ill. pp.170–71). The demons are pulling the damned out of the boat with boathooks and leading them to the judge at the entrance of the underworld, King Minos. He has a snake coiled around him, a reference to the circle of hell to which each of the damned is being relinquished. He also appears as a personification of the verses from the fifth canto of Dante's "Inferno."

The multiplicity of figures and the details portrayed is almost overwhelming and can merely be given mention in this context. Reference should still be made, however, to the attempts at attribution in the literature that concentrate on the portrayal of contemporaries in the picture. Thus, for example, the figure directly behind St. Bartholomew has been thought to be the representation of Michelangelo's assistant Francesco Urbino and Bartholomew's features have been identified with those of Pietro Aretino.

"There stands Minòs grotesquely,
and he snarls,
examining the guilty at the entrance;
he judges and dispatches, tail in coils....

Knows to what place in Hell the soul belongs;
the times he wraps his tail around himself
tells just how far the sinner must go down."

Dante, The Divine Comedy: Inferno, Canto V.

In each of the lunettes (ill. pp.174, 175 and Sistine Chapel fold-out) that complete the painting, moving upward, are depicted wingless angels, holding the symbols of the Passion of Christ: in the left lunette are the Golgotha Cross and the crown of thorns; in the right is the flagellation column that the angels are trying to set up.

Both Michelangelo's biographers and the later Michelangelo literature have emphasized the variety of the emotions shown in the facial expressions and gestures of the figures. It is fear and worry that predominate in the countenances of the risen dead and the flock of the blessed gathered around Christ, rather than joy in the hope of redemption. In the grotesque faces of the monstrous, blood-curdling demons, by contrast, are reflected greed and malice (ill. pp.172–3), while the damned falling into the depths are gripped by despair and fear.

Also highly impressive are the immense kinetic dynamism and the composition of the human body in motion. The figures are portrayed in complicated turning movements, intertwined,

PAGES 168–9
The Last Judgment, detail of the middle lower section with the horde of
trumpet-blowing angels and on the left the group of the risen dead; on
the right the group of the damned and the descent into hell.

The Last Judgment, detail of the lower right section with Charon's boat,
out of which the damned are being pushed, and the demons with King
Minos, who has the features of the papal master of ceremonies Biagio
da Cesena.

In this iconographic detail Michelangelo has drawn very closely on
Dante's *The Divine Comedy*, in which the third canto of the Inferno reads:

"The devil, Charon, with eyes of glowing coals,
summons them all together with a signal,
and with an oar he strikes the laggard sinner."

171

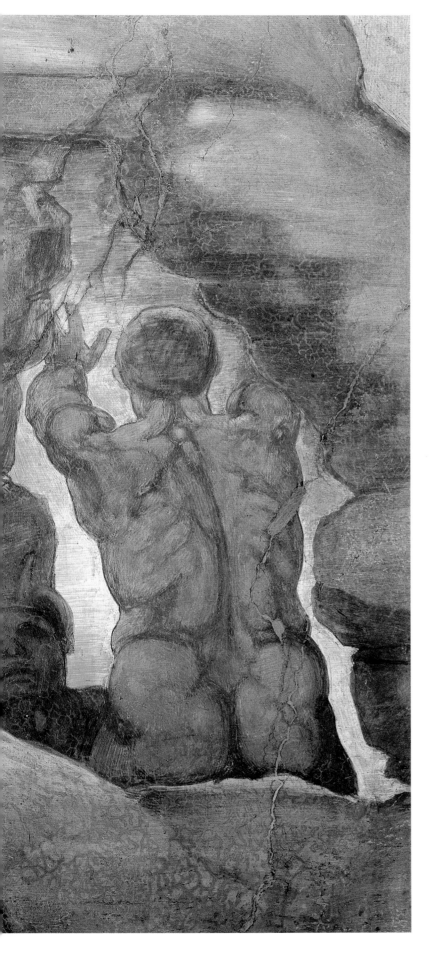

determined by the upward and downward trajectories into the heights or the depths of the painting. The perspectival shortenings, which are very clearly recognizable in the group of sibyls, virgins, and female figures from the Old Testament—they appear on the left side of the picture in the furthest area of the group of the elect, exactly below the lunettes—reinforce the impression of spatial depth. The bodies of the damned and demons, entwined in battle, are reminiscent of the abundance and tension of the figures that already characterized Michelangelo's early centaur relief (ill. pp.18–19). In contrast to this stands the homogeneity of the execution, which is astounding if we consider that Michelangelo worked for at least six years on the fresco that required countless phases of painting that gave rise to hundreds of figures (ill. p.161).

Michelangelo's confident, creative power, with which he also breaks away from the established tradition in the portrayal of the Last Judgment, becomes visible from a few innovations in the pictorial construction, as well as in the iconography of individual motifs. Thus, he overcomes the strict geometrical arrangement of the figures that had previously characterized representations of the Last Judgment, if we think for example of Giotto's frescoes in the Scrovegni Chapel in Padua, and breaks through to a lively composition that is imbued with the most various lines of movement in the figures. Christ appears as a world judge who is no longer seated among the apostles on a throne in the clouds, as described in Matthew's Gospel. Michelangelo's departure from the traditional iconography can also be discerned in the portrayal of damnation.

While on the one hand the unveiling of the painting filled contemporaries with the greatest astonishment with regard to the artistic achievement, on the other hand some highly critical voices were also raised to the effect that the work was obscene and scandalous. In the wake of the revival of Catholic doctrine at the Council of Trent, the attacks of contemporaries intensified; Michelangelo was even reproached with heresy. One of the fiercest critics proved to be Pietro Aretino, who in a defamatory letter in November 1545 maliciously remarked, "Is it possible that you, who, since you are divine, do not condescend to consort with human beings, have done this in the greatest temple built to God…. Your art would be at home in some voluptuous bagnio, certainly not in the highest chapel of the world…. Up to the present time the splendor of such

The Last Judgment, detail of the lower section with the demonic creature between the risen dead and the pit of hell.

"Everything I see is sheer terror, and this terror is connected with the ceiling. On this wall, the human being is still naked, and yet now he is the measure of nothing. Everything has changed. The Renaissance and its spirit are over. The Inquisition is gaining ground. Everywhere fear has suppressed hope…. There is no longer any dream alive in these bodies, no matter how wonderful they once were. Only anger and repentance remain" (Berger).

The Last Judgment, detail of the upper left lunette with angels who are setting up the Golgotha Cross. Vatican, Sistine Chapel, altar wall, Rome.

audacious marvels hath not gone unpunished; for their very superexcellence is the death of your good name" (Addington Symonds). Aretino's fierce attack was only one of the polemics and defamations directed at Michelangelo's painting, which even became a matter for the Council of Trent. Even while Michelangelo was still working on *The Last Judgment*, the papal master of ceremonies Biagio da Cesena put forward some censorship proposals. When he saw the fresco in its already advanced state with Pope Paul III, Biagio disparagingly declared it to be "most disgraceful that in such a sacred place those nude figures should have been depicted all exposing themselves so shamefully" and said that the work belonged not in the pope's chapel but in "the public baths or taverns." This is supposed to have so enraged Michelangelo that he painted the master of ceremonies "in the figure of Minos, shown with a great serpent curled round his legs, among a heap of devils in hell" (Vasari).

The greatest danger for the painting, however, proceeded from the Carafa Pope Paul IV (1555–59). He was considering plans to extend the Sistine Chapel toward the Sacristy, which would have entailed the destruction of *The Last Judgment*. He had already previously asked Michelangelo to cover the naked areas of his figures, to which Michelangelo made a highly sarcastic response: "Tell the pope that this is a trivial matter and can be easily arranged; let him set about putting the world to rights, for the pictures are soon put right" (Vasari). During Pius V's pontificate, the Congregation of the Council of Trent decided, on January 11, 1564, to have the private parts of the bodies painted over.

The commission for this was given of all people to Daniele da Volterra (ca. 1509–66), who was a friend of Michelangelo's. He painted over the incriminated naked areas of the nude figures with so-called *braghe* (breeches), which brought

The Last Judgment, detail of the upper right lunette with angels who are setting up the flagellation column. Vatican, Sistine Chapel, altar wall, Rome.

him the ignominious nickname *braghettone*, the breeches-maker, with which he has entered art history. In 1565, he also repainted the figures of St. Blasius and St. Catherine, altering their postures. In the restoration works on *The Last Judgment* it emerged that he both used the *buon fresco* technique, applying the colors to the still damp wall-plaster, and carried out some of the overpaintings of naked parts of the body *a secco*, applying the paint directly to the plaster that had already dried (ill. pp.166–7).

The Michelangelo expert Pierluigi de Vecchi regarded both the radical criticisms and the words of praise as an expression of the same bewilderment toward a work that could not fail to disturb contemporaries by its violation of "all the fundamental rules of Renaissance art," as well as the abandonment of the rigorously architectonic structure. The events in the picture are no longer dominated by order and moderation: the dynamic

and impetuous representation of the figures and "the systematic exaggeration of gestures and movements" are seen by De Vecchi as the crucial factor in the reaction of contemporaries who found the work intolerable, but he also saw the deeper meaning of *The Last Judgment* as consisting in its depiction of "the shipwreck of entire tormented and suffering humanity… anxiously awaiting the fulfillment of the promise that in the presence of Christ the Judge and Redeemer the righteous will rise from the dead at the end of time" (Vecchi).

In this notion of redemption through Christ's sacrificial death, *The Last Judgment* is revealed as an expression of the reformist thinking with which Michelangelo had become familiar through the reform circle of the "Spirituali" around Vittoria Colonna (ill. p.178), the marchioness of Pescara. The documents give only imprecise information about how the association between the artist and the marchioness

Unknown Florentine sixteenth-century artist, *Portrait of Vittoria Colonna*. Oil on wood, 22¾ x 16¾ in. (58 x 42.5 cm). Casa Buonarroti, Florence.

*"If it is true, lady, that though divine
in beauty you can act like any mortal being,
who still lives and eats and sleeps and
speaks here among us, then not
to follow you when, thanks to
your grace and mercy, all doubt
on this has ceased—what punishment
would be sufficient for such a sin?
For anyone who relies on
his own thoughts, using
the eye that does not
see, is slow to love through his own
power. Form in me a shape from outside,
as I do on stone or on a blank sheet,
which in itself contains nothing,
and then has there what I wish."*

*Poem by Michelangelo to Vittoria Colonna,
thought to date from 1536.*

developed. It is known, however, that already in 1531 Vittoria was asking for a work by Michelangelo, which was in vain, however. Few letters from their rich correspondence have been preserved; the letters from 1538 that have come down to us show that they were in lively contact at this time.

Vittoria Colonna, who came from one of the most highly respected noble Roman families, had left Rome after the death of her husband, the margrave of Pescara, in May 1541, and lived from the end of 1541 to 1544 in the convent of Santa Caterina in Viterbo, where Michelangelo often visited her and they exchanged their thoughts. In many poems dedicated to her, Michelangelo expressed his deep reverence and Platonic love for the marchioness, one of the most learned and influential women in sixteenth-century Italy. In a poem he wrote in 1536 (see p.178), Michelangelo praises Vittoria's beauty, on which he confers supernal traits.

Vittoria Colonna was the only woman in the Spirituali reform circle who was seeking the revival of belief and reform of the Church—with the goal of reconciliation between Protestantism and the Catholic Church. In the papal curia, the circle found followers in Cardinals Reginald Pole (1500–58), Giovanni Morone (1509–80), and Gasparo Contarini (1483–1542), as well as Pole's collaborators Marcantonio Flaminio, Alvise Priuli, and Ludovico Beccadelli. Michelangelo was a friend of the humanist and diplomat Beccadelli (1501–72), who was appointed Bishop of Ravello in 1548 and Archbishop of Ragusa in 1555, until his death.

The ideas of the reform circle were based on the article of faith that redemption depended not on good works, considered to be less important, but purely on belief. The group to which Michelangelo belonged from 1543 was persecuted for heresy following the Council of Trent and the Inquisition, which was gathering force in the period of the Counter-Reformation. Cardinal Gian Pietro Carafa, later Paul IV, battled doggedly from the 1540s against the adherents of the circle, whom he considered to be dangerous heretics who represented a threat to the official church. And Gian Pietro was finally able to triumph: The circle of the Spirituali dissolved. This background

PAGES 176–7
The Last Judgment, detail of the middle lower section with the trumpet-blowing angels and one of the damned, who is being embraced by the demons so as to snatch him into the abyss, and more of the damned on the right.

▷ Sketches for *The Last Judgment* with Michelangelo's signature, 1536–41. Black chalk, 15¼ x 10 in. (38.7 x 25.4 cm). British Museum, London.

Mice Angelo Buonaroti

Jacopino del Conte, *Portrait of Michelangelo Buonarroti*, ca. 1535. Oil on canvas, 38¾ x 26¾ in. (98.5 x 68 cm). Casa Buonarroti, Florence.

is important for an understanding of Michelangelo's last great painting commission: the frescoes for the Pauline Chapel.

"I SHALL PAINT ILL-CONTENT..."—THE PAULINE CHAPEL FRESCOES

Michelangelo had scarcely completed work on *The Last Judgment* and returned to the sculptures for the still unfinished Julius tomb when Pope Paul III entrusted him with a further commission: the painting of the Pauline Chapel in the Vatican. This commission meant that a further postponement to the end of the "tragedy" surrounding the tomb for Julius II could be anticipated. In the letters from this period, Michelangelo with some bitterness expressed his fear of being unable to fulfill the contract he had signed in 1532 with the Della Rovere heirs for the completion of the tomb. To Piergiovanni Aliotti, Paul III's Master of the Robes, he wrote very obstinately: "But to return to the painting. It is not in my power to refuse Pope Paolo anything. I shall paint ill-content, and shall produce things that

are ill-contenting." His objections were of no avail; he had to bow to the pope's wishes.

Michelangelo was sixty-seven years old when he reluctantly started work on the frescoes at the end of 1542. These were to decorate the side walls of the Pauline Chapel, which had been built by Antonio da Sangallo the Younger in 1537 under commission from Paul III, not far from the Sistine Chapel.

Francesco Urbino worked as Michelangelo's assistant in the painting of this chapel, as previously with *The Last Judgment*, and one of the tasks he was given was to prepare the colors. Although the painted surface of the two frescoes is many times smaller than that of *The Last Judgment*—each of the pictures measuring "only" 20½ feet (6.25 meters) high and 21½ feet (6.6 meters) wide—they occupied Michelangelo for a period of at least eight years. The precise background to the origination of the frescoes is only incompletely recorded. However, we must first consider the interruptions to the work by Michelangelo's severe illnesses in summer 1544 and around the turn of the year 1545/1546, which delayed the completion of the earliest fresco, *The Conversion of Paul*, until the summer of 1545 (ill. p.181), with the next, *The Crucifixion of Peter*, originating supposedly from early 1546 and being completed in 1550, perhaps early in that year (ill. p.183).

Both works have been treated as orphans in the annals of art history; the art criticism of the eighteenth and nineteenth centuries in particular could hardly begin to engage with them. They were repeatedly seen as evidence of the artist's failing creative powers, caused by his physical age, which is already refuted by the fact that Michelangelo was able as an architect to design the greatest buildings and to direct their execution in the years that followed. It was not until the first half of the twentieth century that these late paintings of Michelangelo's received due attention.

Detailed consideration of the pictures again reveals Michelangelo's virtuoso creative power in the representation of movement, as well as his unique gift for depicting the events credibly and addressing the viewer directly. At the same time—in the composition and the details of the picture, reminiscent here of *The Last Judgment*—we can recognize a departure from the rigorous construction and symmetry of the conventional canon of forms of Renaissance painting.

In *The Conversion of Paul*, Michelangelo depicts that moment when Saul, lying on the ground having fallen from his horse, is converted to Paul by a bolt of lightning. In the sky above on the left can be seen the Christ figure, from whom, as a sign of divine grace, a yellow ray of light is proceeding. The central events are moved away from the middle axis to the left of the picture in a revolutionary way. Some iconographic innovations are also revealed in the detail, for instance in the protagonists Christ and Paul. The latter is portrayed here, contrary to tradition, as an old man and furthermore in simple garments, without lavishly decorated armor indicating that he is a soldier

The Conversion of Paul, 1542–45.
Fresco, 246 x 259¾ in. (625 x 660 cm).
Vatican, Pauline Chapel, Rome.

Michelangelo portrayed Saul converted to Paul as an old man, contrary
to the iconographic tradition. Michelangelo research has discerned the
features of Michelangelo in the bearded figure.

(ill. p.185); Christ is shown not majestically on a throne in the
clouds, but shooting the lightning headfirst from the sky. In
the soldier figures, Michelangelo has renounced any military
attributes, completely unlike Raphael, for example. Thus, a
tapestry that goes back to a sketch by Raphael—at the basis
of this lies the cartoon made by Raphael in 1514–15 for a wall
hanging in the Sistine Chapel (now in the Vatican Museum)—
shows groups of soldiers armed with lances, equipped with
swords and armor (ill. p.182, left).

In *The Crucifixion of Peter*, Michelangelo also reveals
a departure from the established iconographic tradition
(ill. p.183). This is attested by a comparison with the treatment
of the subject by the Florentine painter Filippino Lippi
(ca. 1475–1504). In his *Crucifixion of Peter*—one of the Peter
frescoes he completed in 1481–83 (begun ca. 1424 by Masolino) in
the Brancacci Chapel in Santa Maria del Carmine in Florence—
Lippi portrays the crucified martyr static and defenseless, with
head hanging down nailed to the inverted Cross (ill. p.182,

right). In a rigorously symmetrical iconographic construction, the Cross here stands precisely in the vertical of the middle axis of the picture, whereas Michelangelo breaks up this symmetry with the diagonal of the Cross.

Michelangelo's innovations continue in further details of the picture. Whereas in Lippi Peter is portrayed in the role of the defenseless, passive martyr, in Michelangelo's fresco he is characterized by activity. This is visible in Peter's bent bodily posture, as he stretches his upper body upward in a strained movement, with raised head, turning toward the viewer with an energetic, accusatory gaze. Even the treatment of the topography of the historical events reveals a departure from tradition. While in Lippi the architecture of medieval Rome can be recognized in the background, in Michelangelo's *Crucifixion* there are no references at all to historical location. In *The Conversion of Paul*, the historical site of the events, the city of Damascus, is vaguely indicated in the right background of the picture, whereas in *The Crucifixion of Peter* the landscape is completely devoid of any local integration; we no longer see anything but an abstract hilly landscape. This is a significant indication of the temporally situated iconographic language. In this departure from historical context, the inherent meaning

lower half of the picture this dynamism proceeds from the various trajectories of the groups of soldiers. The light, which is characterized by a subtler graduation of the chiaroscuro contrasts, compared with the previous harsh contrasts in *The Last Judgment*, is introduced by Michelangelo for the specific purpose of concentration on the central events. In *The Conversion of Paul* the diffuse light of the bolt-ray falling from the top left produces a connection between Christ and Paul and thus emphasizes the activity of the protagonists. In *The Crucifixion of Peter*, the light is directed onto the martyr standing in the center: With bright luminosity it falls directly onto the body of Peter nailed to the cross and the figures of the men who are setting this up, and thus connects the martyr with his tormentors.

The color is also introduced by Michelangelo in a masterly way to emphasize the events taking place. What is especially remarkable here is the homogeneity of the coloring—if we consider the long gestation period of the works—which in both frescoes is determined by a red–blue–green triad. As in *The Last Judgment*, the costly, cold-radiating lapis lazuli is deployed in the sky area. In *The Conversion of Paul* it forms a lively contrast to the radiance of the red in the garments of Christ and Paul and, in parallel with the light effect,

After Raphael, *The Conversion of St. Paul*, wall hanging from a sketch by Raphael (1514–15) from the workshop in Beauvais, 1695–98. Cathedral, Beauvais, France.

Filippino Lippi, *The Crucifixion of Peter*, 1481–82. Fresco, 90½ x 235½ in. (230 x 598 cm). Santa Maria del Carmine, Brancacci Chapel, Florence.

of the iconographic events is conveyed as a message of belief that works supertemporally—the message of an act of redemption that is directly addressing the viewer not in the past but the present.

In both pictures an extraordinary dynamism is given to the events: In *The Conversion of Paul* it proceeds from the group of wingless angels revolving around Christ in the upper left region of the picture, which are reminiscent of the figures from the group of the elect in *The Last Judgment*; in the

connects the main figures. In some of the soldiers' garments, it accentuates the dynamism of their diverging movements. In *The Crucifixion of Peter* everything is outshone by the bright figure of the martyr at the center of the picture. Here the blue, red, and gold-yellow color tones of the figures emphasize the dynamic turning movement that takes place among the intertwined arms of the tormentors.

The frescoes of the Pauline Chapel, which Michelangelo completed at the advanced age of seventy-five years, were

The Crucifixion of Peter, 1546–50. Fresco, 246 x 260¼ in. (625 x 661 cm).
Vatican, Pauline Chapel, Rome.

his last works in the domain of painting. As he himself expressed it to Vasari, they "cost him a great deal of effort," the demands of fresco painting being "no work for old men who have passed a certain age" (Vasari). In fact, they remained the completed part of a design that included further paintings and for which the cartoons had already been made. After the death of the patron, Pope Paul III, on November 10, 1549, however, the works were discontinued, so the planned design was never executed.

The Conversion of Paul and *The Crucifixion of Peter* are an expression of spirituality, the new religious sensibility that characterized Michelangelo's creative work from the early 1540s in his engagement with the reformist ideas of the Spirituali around Vittoria Colonna, Cardinals Pole, Morone, Contarini, and others. Thus, the frescoes can be read as symbols of the pure belief in Christ and the hope of redemption on this same foundation. The art historian Fritz Baumgart also sees this essence of Michelangelo's transformation, which

183

> "So it transpires that it is no mistake to be slower, if necessary, even very slow indeed, and to spend a great deal of time and effort on a work, if it becomes more perfect as a result. The only thing that is blameworthy is poor achievement—not accomplishing something."
>
> *Michelangelo in conversation with Francisco de Hollanda about his mastery and working method in painting.*

manifests itself in the style of the artworks of his old age, as expressed primarily in *The Crucifixion of Peter*. Compared with *The Conversion of Paul*, he suggests that in this "a new, deeper feeling of belief has found expression that is also expressed in the poems of this period and the following one." In the place of redemption by the raging and punishing God of the Last Judgment and *The Conversion of Paul* has "emerged elevation by the loving and suffering God" (Baumgart/Biagetti).

In that late sonnet, which begins with the famous lines "My life's journey has finally arrived," perhaps the most moving of Michelangelo's poems, the last stanza brings to expression the notion of redemption that is implicit in *The Crucifixion of Peter*. This thought was to find a final progression in the late *Pietà* representations. "Neither painting nor sculpting can any longer quieten my soul, turned now to that divine love which on the Cross, to embrace us, opened wide its arms."

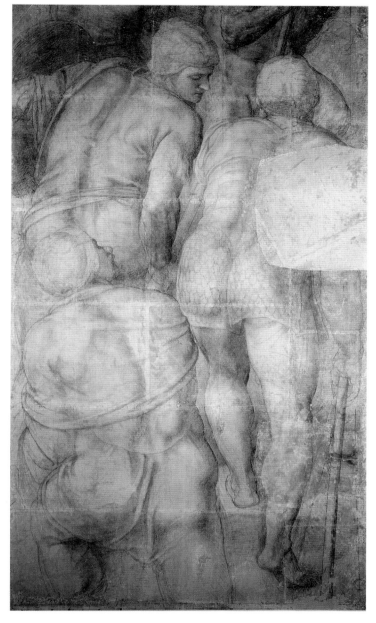

Group of Soldiers, fragment of the cartoon for *The Crucifixion of Peter*, ca. 1546.
Black chalk with wash, heightened with white, 103¼ x 61½ in. (262 x 155.9 cm).
Museo Nazionale di Capodimonte, Naples.

◁ *The Crucifixion of Peter*, 1546–50.
Fresco, 246 x 260¼ in. (625 x 661 cm).
Vatican, Pauline Chapel, Rome.

In the pilgrim figure at the lower right border of the picture, Michelangelo is also thought to have painted his self-portrait. That could be interpreted as a declaration of his renewed religious faith in the later years of his life.

THE NEW CONSTRUCTION OF ST. PETER'S IN ROME

THE LARGEST CHURCH IN CHRISTENDOM

"In its ponderous peace, Michelangelo's dome on St. Peter's in Rome gives the impression of that stony eternity with which the *Roma aeterna* as a whole is associated. Completed in May 1590, sixteen years after Michelangelo's death, it appears as the symbol of an era that was predestined to fashion something universally valid for all time out of the consensus of all concerned. But this impression is false. Like St. Peter's as a whole, the dome was not the result of long-term planning based on authoritative artistic standards but the product of relentlessly battling rival projects" (Bredekamp). With this insight, Horst Bredekamp introduces his highly informative study of the tortuous and difficult architectural history of the new construction of St. Peter's. The following account, tracing three centuries of the architectural history of the most important church in Catholic Christendom, focuses on the construction phases that were carried out under the aegis of Michelangelo. They formed part of the history of a vast number of designs by the most important architects that were subject to the alternation between agreement, modification, and replacement for which Bredekamp coined the metaphor of a "pendulum-swing of demolition and construction."

The new construction of St. Peter's was directly interwoven with Michelangelo's creative work at the latest from 1505, although the search for an appropriate installation site for the tomb of the Della Rovere Pope Julius II had provided the impetus for the new construction, for which Julius II commissioned Donato Bramante (1444–1514), Michelangelo's unpleasant rival, in 1506 (ill. p.190). Bramante's plan envisaged the erection of a central-plan building with a central crossing cupola with four lower cupolas and four towers, as well as large choir ambulatories in the west that would have resulted in the

demolition at least of the western section of the old St. Peter's. This, the first St. Peter's, a five-aisle basilica with a flat ceiling, a single-nave transept, and a western apse, had been built by Emperor Constantine the Great at the beginning of the fourth century over St. Peter's grave, which was then consecrated in AD 326 by Pope Sylvester I.

Toward the middle of the fifteenth century, under Pope Nicholas V's pontificate (1447–55) endeavors had already been made to extend the old Constantinian basilica by building a large choir in the western apse. These plans, however, on which the architects Bernardo Rossellino (1409–64) and Leon Battista Alberti (1404–72) had worked, came to a standstill, and only those for the foundations of the new choir had progressed. This was the situation that Michelangelo encountered in 1505 when searching for an installation site for the Julius tomb, which led Julius II to announce a competition for a new construction of St. Peter's that was won by Bramante.

The laying of the foundation stone for the new construction undertaken by Bramante followed on April 18, 1506. Bramante, who began his work with the demolition of the western apse of the Constantinian basilica and the construction of the choir, envisaged the ideal solution for the new construction of St. Peter's as a central-plan building with large choir ambulatories to be constructed on the ground plan of a Greek cross; later, however, he returned to the idea of extending the nave so that the new building would include the sacred domain of the old Constantinian basilica. The central, hemispherically designed cupola—for which Bramante's inspiration had been the cupola of the Pantheon—was to become an architectonic symbol of the triumphant church and the powerful papacy.

From 1506 to 1511, Bramante drove the project forward. This construction phase saw the origination of the four massive cupola piers that were built in the western section, over which the central crossing cupola was to be erected. However, the works dragged on and on, not least because Julius II drastically cut the financial resources for the new construction. After Bramante's death in 1514, the supervision of the building work was taken over by Raphael (until 1520), Baldassare Peruzzi (until 1537), and from 1538/39 until his death in 1546 Antonio da Sangallo the Younger. In this period, the plans changed from a nave building, based on the ground plan of a Latin cross, to the

PAGES 186–7
St. Peter's, Rome, New building, 1506, interior view of the cupola (Michelangelo's plan of 1547, completed 1593 by Giacomo della Porta) and upper lintel of the canopy over St. Peter's tomb (by Gian Lorenzo Bernini, 1624–33). Vatican, St. Peter's, Rome.

▷ St. Peter's, Rome, New building, 1506, external view of the cupola and the fascia from the west, Vatican, St. Peter's, Rome.

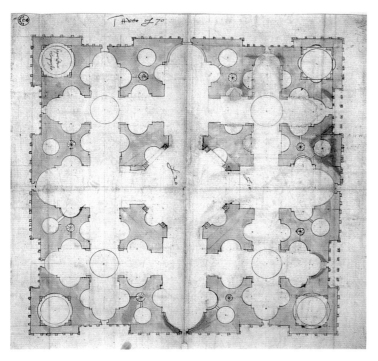

Giuliano da Sangallo, Ground plan drawing for the new St. Peter's, 1506.
Pen with wash.
Folio 8A r, Gabinetto dei Disegni e delle Stampe degli Uffizi, Florence.

These two plan sketches appear on the verso and recto pages of a folio. Horst Bredekamp sees Bramante's sketch as a reaction to the central-plan design of his collaborator Sangallo and evidence for the thesis that in the earlier construction phase Bramante did not envisage an entirely central-plan building because he extended the building eastward into a nave.

Donato Bramante, Ground plan sketch for the new St. Peter's, 1506.
Pen with wash.
Folio 8A v, Gabinetto dei Disegni e delle Stampe degli Uffizi, Florence.

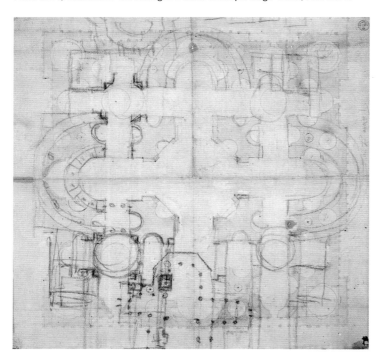

conception of a central-plan building, founded on the ground plan of a Greek cross.

When Pope Paul III transferred the construction supervision of St. Peter's to Michelangelo after Sangallo's death in 1546, Michelangelo decided in favor of Bramante's original conception of the central-plan building. In a letter addressed not unambiguously "To Bartolommeo," that Michelangelo wrote between the end of 1546 and early 1547, probably to Bartolommeo Ferratini, bishop and head of the supervision of St. Peter's construction under Paul III, he made the following statement, which included some brusque criticism, especially of Sangallo: "Messer Bartolommeo, dear friend—One cannot deny that Bramante was as skilled in architecture as anyone since the time of the ancients. He it was who laid down the first plan of St. Peter's, not full of confusion, but clear, simple, luminous, and detached in such a way that it in no wise impinged upon the Palace. It was held to be a beautiful design, and manifestly still is, so that anyone who has departed from Bramante's arrangement, as Sangallo has done, has departed from the true course; and that this is so can be seen by anyone who looks at his model with unprejudiced eyes."

Sangallo's model, which is known to us from an engraving of 1546 by Antonio Labacco with the exterior view from the north, was rejected by Michelangelo with a cynical comment in the same letter because the building had "no light of its own" and "so many dark, lurking places above and below that they afford ample opportunity for innumerable disgraces, such as the hiding of exiles, the coining of base money, the raping of nuns, and other rascalities." Furthermore, Michelangelo believed Sangallo's model would necessitate the demolition of parts of the existing architecture, so that the Pauline Chapel, the rooms of the keeper of the papal seal and the Rota Romana (court of the Apostolic See) and even the Sistine Chapel would not have been spared.

Michelangelo reduced Sangallo's vast model (ill. p.191); he expressed criticism not only of the inadequate consideration of light, but above all also the intricacy of the Sangallo plan. Thus, as Vasari describes, he criticized the numerous rows of columns piled on top of each other and the countless "projections, spires, and subdivisions of members" with which Sangallo departed from the "sound method of the ancient world." He observed not without a hint of malice that in the execution of the building "fifty years of time and over three hundred thousand crowns of money" could be saved while still achieving "more majesty, grandeur, and facility, better ordered design, and greater beauty and convenience" (Vasari). As Vasari goes on to report, Michelangelo proved the truth of his words in a model that he prepared within two weeks. Michelangelo's master plan for the design of the new building has only been preserved from an engraving by Étienne Dupérac (ill. p.192).

Returning to Bramante's central-plan building idea, Michelangelo planned a simplification and streamlining of

Wooden model of St. Peter's Basilica from a 1516 plan
by Antonio Sangallo the Younger. Vatican, Vatican Museums, Rome.

the construction. He ordered the demolition of one part of the structure that had already been erected under Sangallo, canceled Sangallo's detailed module additions and broke through to a monumental structure that can be seen very clearly from the wall structure of the western apse (ill. p.193): mighty travertine paired pilasters, connected by an entablature projecting from the wall, decorating the apses and the corners of the cross-shaped arms of the square ground plan, as well as the diagonally arranged piers between apses and corners (Bredekamp). The monumental structure of the double pilasters gives the main body of the building plasticity and also a vertical trajectory that is supported by the gable-crowned tabernacles that are closely set between them. The plastically animated structure of the external building inspired the art historian William E. Wallace to make a comparison with geological movements; Michelangelo has invented "a form of tectonic geology": "The walls behave like tectonic plates that push into each other and rub against each other" (Wallace).

One of the most important alterations to the Sangallo model was made by Michelangelo through the inclusion of light, which also manifested itself in the formation of the cupola (ill. p.195). Thus, the drum is crossed by a row of sixteen windows that allow light to fall into the central church interior over St. Peter's tomb. Between 1558 and 1561, at the instigation of his followers Michelangelo created the wooden model of the cupola for which he had been inspired by the cupola of Florence Cathedral built by Filippo Brunelleschi (1377–1446). The large diameter of the cupola—measuring around 138 feet (42 meters)—presented a special challenge for stability (ill. p.194). The solution consisted of absorbing the powerful pressure of the cupola vault and transferring it to the four powerful, five-sided pier buttresses of the crossing.

At Michelangelo's death, the cupola was completed only as far as the drum. The above-mentioned copperplate engraving by Dupérac conveys the intentions that Michelangelo was pursuing here. He rejected Sangallo's densely packed rows

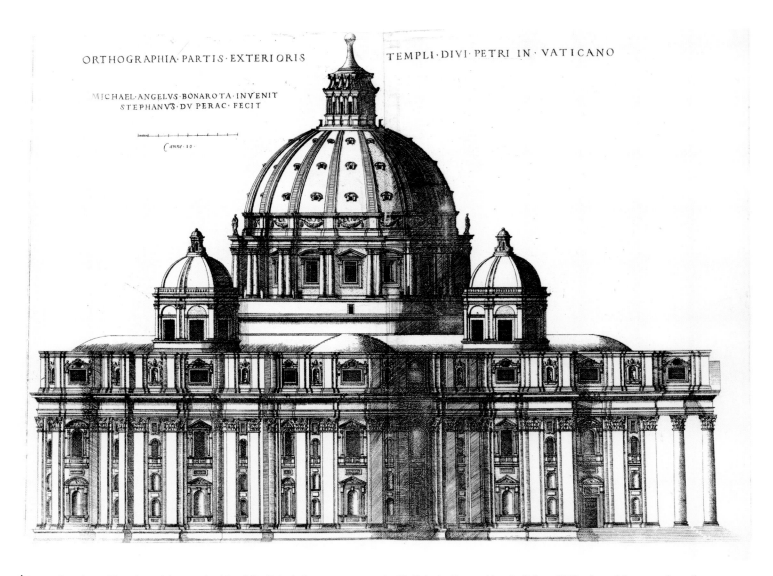

ORTHOGRAPHIA·PARTIS·EXTERIORIS   TEMPLI·DIVI·PETRI·IN·VATICANO

MICHAEL·ANGELVS·BONAROTA·INVENIT
STEPHANVS·DV·PERAC·FECIT

Canne·10·

Étienne Dupérac, Elevation of the south side of St. Peter's from Michelangelo's sketch, from "Orthographia partis exterioris (&) interioris Templi Divi Petri in Vaticano," ca. 1577. Copperplate engraving. Private collection.

▷ St. Peter's, Rome, New building, 1506, view of the apse from the southwest.

of arcades and returned to Bramante's hemispherical design of the cupola, in which the drum was to be surrounded by a classical-style colonnade of columns. Here, too, the backward and forward projection of architectural elements, the powerful paired columns with—in contrast to Bramante's conception— broken entablature and the windows projecting back between them reveal the organic plasticity that characterizes Michelangelo's architectural language.

PAGE 194
St. Peter's, Rome, New building, 1506, interior view of the cupola (Michelangelo's sketch of 1547, completed 1593 by Giacomo della Porta) and the canopy over St. Peter's grave (by Gian Lorenzo Bernini, 1624–33). Vatican, St. Peter's, Rome.

PAGE 195
Michelangelo, Giacomo della Porta, and Luigi Vanvitelli,
Original wooden model of the cupola of St. Peter's, 1558–61. Vatican Museums, Sala dell'Immacolata, Rome.

The cupola rises over the drum that is divided by sixteen ribs that ascend powerfully to the lantern, which is itself enclosed by double columns. The cupola was completed from 1588 to 1590 with an alteration to Michelangelo's established proportions by Giacomo della Porta (ca. 1540 to 1602) and Domenico Fontana (1543–1607). Della Porta raised the cupola shell by several meters, intensifying its upward movement, while also reducing the height of the lantern. Otherwise the exterior composition designed by Michelangelo was maintained, so that the planned changes to the effect of the cupola would not harm anything.

Apart from Della Porta and Fontana, further architects were commissioned with the construction supervision of St. Peter's after Michelangelo's death: in August 1564, Pirro Ligorio, who was responsible for the high fascia of the external façade; following his dismissal in 1566/67 Giacomo (Jacopo) Barozzi da Vignola, who designed the lower cupolas and completed the transept aligned to the north and south; and finally Carlo

Farnese Palace, inner courtyard, second story designed 1517 by Antonio da Sangallo the Younger; upper story by Michelangelo.

After Sangallo's death in 1546, Michelangelo took over the construction supervision at the Farnese Palace and created with his work on it until 1549 one of the most magnificent palaces in Rome. After Michelangelo's death in 1564, the building was completed by Giacomo da Vignola and, from 1575, by Giacomo della Porta.

Maderno, a nephew of Domenico Fontana, and Gian Lorenzo Bernini. In the wake of the innovations introduced by the Council of Trent for the Christian liturgy, Michelangelo's design of the central-plan building under Pope Paul V (1605–21) was finally to be modified into a nave building. Carlo Maderno, construction supervisor of the new St. Peter's Basilica from 1603, from 1607 to 1614 extended the central-plan building eastward with a nave and a portico along the façade, which he completed in 1614. In 1626 followed the consecration of the new St. Peter's.

FURTHER ARCHITECTURAL PROJECTS OF THE LATE PERIOD

In addition to the vast project of St. Peter's, Michelangelo worked on a series of further architectural projects, including some secular buildings that resulted from papal commissions. Paul III, the pope from the Farnese family, had while still cardinal in 1524 commissioned Antonio da Sangallo the Younger with the

redesign and expansion of the Farnese Palace. After Sangallo's death in 1546, Michelangelo took over the continuation of the construction, which was then only to be completed in 1589, twenty-five years after his death. The palace, which became the residence of the cardinals Ranuccio and Odoardo Farnese, the nephews of Paul III, was considered the most splendid cardinal's palace in Rome (ill. p.196).

In its general architectonic conception, the building is reminiscent of the type represented by the palaces in Florence, but it contains one striking difference in the composition of the façade: the extensive rusticated masonry of the Florentine façades is replaced here by a brick face and the rustication is restricted to the powerful quoins. The façade is plastically divided by the horizontal rows of the cornices that separate the three stories of the building, as well as the framed, gable-crowned windows. At the top, the building is completed by a powerful, overhanging crowning cornice. The architectonic structure combines peace and animation in a harmonious total effect. In an alteration to Sangallo's plans, Michelangelo

Palazzo dei Conservatori, front view, 1564–86, built from plans by
Michelangelo, executed by Giacomo della Porta.
Piazza del Campidoglio, Rome.

"On the southern side, to bring the Conservators' Palace into line he
designed for it a richly adorned façade, with a portico at the foot filled
with columns and niches for many ancient statues; and all around are
various adornments of doors and windows, some of which are already
in place" (Vasari).

introduced the rusticated middle portal and widened the
plastically developed window in the first story, over which
he placed the Farnese marble coat-of-arms. He also raised the
upper story by 10 feet (3 meters) and enlarged the crowning
cornice. As previously in the architecture of the Laurentian
Library (see ill. p.146), here, too, the emancipated treatment of
individual architectural elements is discernible in the portal
wedged between the side windows and the balcony window
crowned by the Farnese coat-of-arms, a signal that prefigures
Mannerism. In the inner courtyard of the palace (ill. p.196)
the three stories are decorated with pillars and columns;
here Michelangelo added the upper story. Vasari even
considered the inner courtyard to be the most beautiful
courtyard in the whole of Europe, with its "incomparably
beautiful, graceful, and varied windows, ornamentation, and
crowning cornice."

The most extensive project after St. Peter's, which occupied
Michelangelo from 1538, was the development of the Capitol
Square, the Piazza del Campidoglio, framed by three powerful

palatial buildings on the Capitoline Hill (ill. pp. 197, 198). The
commission for this new development had again been given
to Michelangelo by Pope Paul III. The bronze equine statue
of the Roman Emperor *Marcus Aurelius* was to be placed in
the very center of the square. The statue, which had survived
from the Middle Ages because it had been mistaken for the
image of the Christian Emperor Constantine I, the Great, was
regarded as the symbol of authority and power of the emperors
of antiquity, to which the popes were now staking their claim.
The statue, therefore, represented a link between antique and
Christian Rome—a new Roman forum also originated as a
papal commission.

Michelangelo's design of the oval plinth for the statue has
a parallel in the tiered oval pavement inside the square, into
which a twelve-pointed star has been set; this refers to the
celestial globe with the twelve signs of the zodiac. In his design,
Michelangelo had to consider two preexisting buildings, the
Palazzo dei Senatori, built in the Middle Ages, and the Palazzo
dei Conservatori, originating from the fifteenth century. They

CAPITOLII · SCIOGRAPHIA · EX · IPSO · EXEMPLARI · MICHAELIS · ANGELI · BONAROTI · A · STEPHANO · DVPERAC · PARISIENSI · ACCVRATE · DELINEATA ET · IN · LVCEM · AEDITA · ROMAE · ANNO · SALVTIS · ∞ ÐLXIX

Étienne Dupérac, Total view of the Piazza del Campodoglio (Capitol Square), Rome, according to Michelangelo's plans, 1569.
Copperplate engraving.
Graphische Sammlung Albertina, Vienna.

▷ San Giovanni dei Fiorentini, Rome, view of the façade completed by Alessandro Galilei in 1734 and the crossing cupola by Carlo Maderno.

Pope Leo X founded the Florentine National Church in Rome. The building that was begun in 1518 and repeatedly interrupted was the work of various architects, including Michelangelo in 1559.

had been built slightly on a diagonal to each other. Michelangelo took account of this when he placed his new building, the Palazzo Nuovo (constructed 1603–55) opposite the Palazzo dei Conservatori as a counterpart. This gave rise to an entire trapezoid area of the square surrounded by three mighty palatial buildings, with the Palazzo dei Senatori on the narrow side. An impression of the whole ensemble of this design for the Capitol is conveyed by the copperplate engraving by Étienne Dupérac in 1569 (ill. p.198). With the layout, Michelangelo gave the total effect of the square a great dynamism. From the entrance of the stairway ramp, the square, tapering backward, creates the optical illusion of a space that is extending into the depths.

In his plans for redeveloping the façades of the Palazzi dei Senatori and Conservatori, which were implemented from 1545 to 1605, Michelangelo drew on the antique repertoire of forms. Pilasters decorated with Corinthian capitals, Ionic

columns, and powerful crowning cornices are among the variety of architectural elements featured.

The unique quality of Michelangelo's architectural language and the way in which it points beyond the antique tradition also comes to expression again here in the sophisticated play with classical architectural forms. Thus, the pilasters set in front of the wall and the Ionic columns that Michelangelo designed for the Palazzo dei Conservatori no longer have a load-bearing function, although they create this impression. The architectural elements that are truly load-bearing—arches, piers, and vaults—Michelangelo intentionally concealed. Here is revealed again his unique technical mastery in applying the laws of stability, which enabled him to "play" with the architecture in this way.

From 1559, Michelangelo worked on plan-drawings for the Florentine National Church in Rome, consecrated San Giovanni dei Fiorentini, to its patron saint St. John (ill. p.199).

Its construction had been started in 1518 under commission from the Medici Pope Leo X (1513–21) by the architect Jacopo Sansovino. Several architects subsequently participated in it, including Antonio da Sangallo the Younger and Giacomo della Porta. The wish of the Florentine community to redesign the church led in 1559 to commissioning Michelangelo. There was decisive interest in the project from Duke Cosimo I de' Medici, as evidenced by a letter by Michelangelo of November 1559 to Cosimo in which he considers it an "express command" of the duke's "to turn my attention to the above-mentioned Church of the Florentines" and mentions that he has "already done several designs suited to the site," not without expressing some regret about his age and his bad health.

Ground plan drawing for San Giovanni dei Fiorentini, Nr 124 Ar, 1559.
Black chalk, pen with wash, 16¾ x 14½ in. (42.6 x 37.1 cm).
Casa Buonarroti, Florence.

The three preserved plan-drawings 120 Ar, 121 A, and 124 Ar (ill. p.200) again reflect Michelangelo's wealth of ideas and his dynamic conception of architecture. The latter arises in the view of the Michelangelo expert Daniel Kupper from the fact that Michelangelo here is stacking next to each other "not only masses," "not merely enclosed spaces," but instead generating the impression "that the whole ground plan is emerging from the end of the compasses" (Kupper). In 1562, the project was abandoned for lack of financial resources from the Florentine patrons. From 1583, Giacomo della Porta continued the building and the façade was completed only in 1734 by Alessandro Galilei under commission from Clement XII, but not according to Michelangelo's plans. Wallace considered the church that stands today on the banks of the Tiber a commonplace ruin compared with Michelangelo's dynamic conception, which was never implemented.

Among the final larger architectural commissions on which Michelangelo worked from 1561 until the last year of his life was the construction of the Porta Pia (ill. p.200). During the restoration of the Roman district of the city, which was one of the Medici Pope Pius IV's principal objectives, this gate construction was to form the splendid conclusion at the northern end of the Via Pia, now known as the Via XX Settembre. Pius IV, who succeeded Paul IV to the papal throne in December 1559, was to become the last

papal patron in Michelangelo's life. The construction of the wide, straight-running Via Pia on the Quirinal Hill was among the earliest development measures for the Roman hill that Pius IV introduced.

The Porta Pia designed by Michelangelo was unfinished at his death. The drawings (ill. p.201) were described by Vasari as "very beautiful and lavish," of which "the pope chose the least costly" (Vasari). In the lower section of the gate construction that Michelangelo designed, he again combined classical architectural elements with new motifs. The portal is framed by mighty pilasters and crowned with a segmentally arched gable with a projecting inscribed tablet, as well as volute-like decorative elements that Wallace likened to coiled springs, which form an arresting contrast to the extravagant false windows and the travertine disks that resemble windows. The gable of the Porta Pia that is visible today was not added until the nineteenth century. Michelangelo had planned a triangular crowning gable as a conclusion, returning to the architectural forms of antique temple façades. Also dating back to his design are the two winged figures around the gable of the façade, as well as the papal coat-of-arms for which they create a frame; in it can be seen the six balls or *palle* that are the symbol of the Medici.

Porta Pia, Via XX Settembre, Rome, constructed by Michelangelo 1561–64 under Pope Pius IV, view of the city side.

▷ Plan for the Porta Pia, 1561.
Black chalk, pen, and brown Indian ink, with wash and heightened with white, 17¼ x 11 in. (44.1 x 28.2 cm). Casa Buonarroti, Florence.

"RELIEVED OF A TROUBLESOME AND HEAVY BURDEN…"

"Michelangelo's cupola (140 feet [42.6 meters] wide) is superior in height to that planned by Bramante… externally his cupola probably presents the most beautiful and noble outline ever attained in architecture." The exceptional praise that the Swiss cultural historian Jacob Burckhardt bestowed in *Cicerone* (1904) on the dome of St. Peter's designed by Michelangelo is representative of the unanimous recognition in the Michelangelo literature that to this day recognizes the artist's essential contribution in creating the form of St. Peter's Basilica.

Domenico Cresti da Passignano, *Michelangelo Presents to Pope Paul IV the Model of St. Peter's*, 1618–19.
Oil on canvas, 93 x 55½ in. (236 x 141 cm). Casa Buonarroti, Florence.

Cresti, a late Renaissance painter from Florence, portrays Michelangelo giving the model of St. Peter's Basilica with the cupola he designed to the pope.

When the construction supervision of the Vatican site office was formally transferred to Michelangelo by Pope Paul III on January 1, 1547, he was already seventy-two years old. One of his first official actions was to dismiss the Florentine architect Nanni di Baccio Bigio (ca. 1511–68), Sangallo's former deputy, as well as his assistant Antonio Labacco, who in seven years of work had created the lavish and extremely costly wooden model of the Sangallo plan for the new St. Peter's (ill. p.191). With this act, which was felt to be a humiliation, he had incurred the hatred of Sangallo's disciples, whom he disparaged as "the Sangallo clique" (Vasari). Thus, even from early 1547 he was subjected to attacks and slanders from his rivals, who right up to the last few years of his life did not desist from their plan to force Michelangelo out of the post. While his opponents constantly hoped on the one hand for the old man's demise, on the other they—first and foremost the above-mentioned Nanni di Baccio Bigio—lost no opportunity to discredit him with Pope Paul III. Yet Michelangelo parried all the attempted attacks with his characteristic tenacity; the unshakable protection of Paul III and the regard that he enjoyed with the pope made him practically unassailable.

In October 1549, Paul III issued a *motu proprio*, a papal decree, which guaranteed Michelangelo a free hand in the construction works—for an artist to be given such freedom of action was an unprecedented and unique event. Michelangelo also enjoyed the pope's confidence and support primarily because Paul III trusted the artist to rid the building site of the web of corruption and waste that had grown up around it over the years, not least under Sangallo and his entourage. For this reason, Michelangelo's appointment was a further thorn in the flesh of his adversaries. Paul's successor, Julius III, who took over the papal office in February 1550, also defended Michelangelo's authority. This is reflected in an episode mentioned by the art historian Horst Bredekamp in his detailed account of the construction history of St. Peter's: After Paul III's death at the end of 1549, the building committee immediately confiscated Michelangelo's keys for the building site. The newly elected Pope Julius "furiously arranged, however, as soon as he took office for the immediate surrender of the keys and the continuation of the work according to Michelangelo's ideas" (Bredekamp). Yet the attacks on Michelangelo continued. One of his opponents' strategies was to prevent posts being held by people who enjoyed Michelangelo's trust with the help of the construction authorities; they also reproached him with waste and incompetence. Thus, it was also a severe setback for Michelangelo when in April 1557 parts of the structure in the southern apse had to be dismantled, for which his esteemed construction supervisor, Sebastiano Malenotti, was responsible. Michelangelo himself referred to the misfortune in a letter addressed to Duke Cosimo I de' Medici in May 1557, in which he described how "a mistake has arisen over the vault of the chapel of the king of France, which is unusual and cunningly contrived, and I shall have to take down a great part of what has been done."

With the pontificate of the Carafa Pope Paul IV, who assumed the papal throne in 1555, conditions worsened for Michelangelo to the point of becoming intolerable. The pope, in whose side Michelangelo had long been a thorn because of his connections with the Spirituali circle around Cardinal Reginald Pole, who were regarded as heretics and whom Paul IV was relentlessly persecuting, not only canceled Michelangelo's salary payments; he also appointed one of Michelangelo's arch-enemies—Pirro Ligorio, the architect from Naples—as architect and collaborator on the "Fabbrica di San Pietro." In Florence, Duke Cosimo I de' Medici had heard how Michelangelo was being troubled by the pope and he tried to persuade the artist to return to his home city. In his reaction to the duke's invitation, Michelangelo revealed some fortitude; it was "his" construction site, from which he could and would not part, even if it had been possible for his plans to be substantially altered by others.

Following the death of the Carafa pope, Michelangelo rediscovered in his successor Pius IV (1559–65) a pope who was well-disposed toward him, but the heads of the site office still sought to drive the aged artist out of office. In fact, Michelangelo announced in a letter written to Cardinal Rodolfo Pio da Carpi in Rome on September 13, 1560, that he intended to ask the pope to discharge him from office as soon as possible. Michelangelo's situation worsened again when his arch-enemy Nanni di Baccio Bigio finally became his deputy with support from the construction authorities in 1563. After his appointment, Nanni not only gave arbitrary orders but also sought to use the circumstances in which Cesare Bettini, one of Michelangelo's closest collaborators, died on the construction site, to discredit Michelangelo. In August 1563, the bishop of Forlì's cook murdered Bettini, having caught him *in flagrante* with his wife. Vasari's account of this incident is also an eloquent testimony to the hostilities to which Michelangelo was subjected to until the end, which culminated in this episode. "Michelangelo had been seventeen

years in the construction of St. Peter's, and several times the superintendents had tried to have his authority taken away from him. When they failed in this they sought to oppose him in every other matter, now on one far-fetched pretext and now on another, in the hope that as he was so old that he could do no more they would force him to retire from sheer weariness. Then it happened that the overseer, Cesare da Casteldurante [Bettini], died, and for the sake of the building Michelangelo sent there, while he was looking for a suitable successor, Luigi Gaeta, who was too young but very competent. Some of the deputies had often tried to get Nanni di Baccio Bigio put in charge…and in order to get their own way the same men sent Luigi Gaeta away" (Vasari). Michelangelo, again showing

St. Peter's Square with St. Peter's Basilica and the Vatican. Colored steel engraving, undated (mid-nineteenth century), by Émile Rouargue. Private collection, Paris.

composure and aplomb, afterward made a personal request of Pope Pius IV to discharge him from the post, yet this was exactly not what the pope had in mind. He summoned the building committee again, who intensified their criticisms of Michelangelo, implying that he had made mistakes in the execution of the building, at which the pope ordered an inspection of the building works by Gabrio Serbelloni that went in Michelangelo's favor. The scheming Nanni was then not removed from his activities, but simply removed from the construction site. According to Vasari, even after Michelangelo's death Pius IV is supposed to have decreed that no changes were to be made to Michelangelo's plans. Of course, even this could not prevent the architects responsible for the continuing construction and completion of St. Peter's after Michelangelo from interfering with his plans.

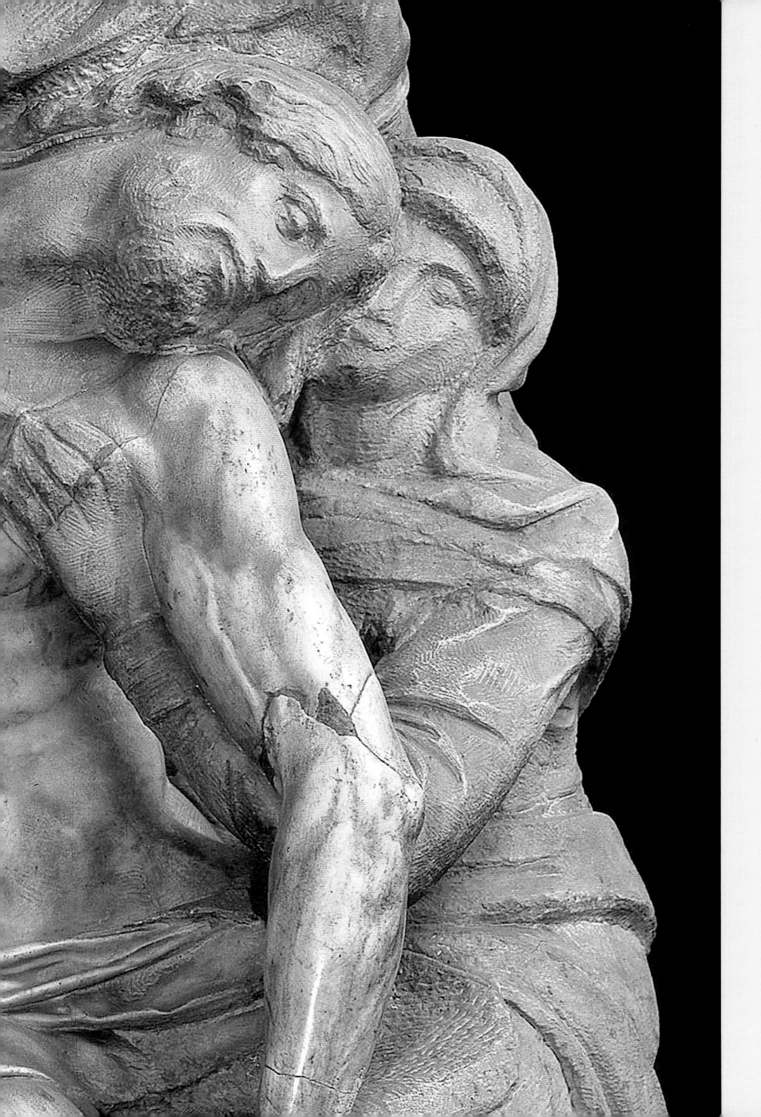

THE LATE WORK

THE CRUCIFIXION AND LAMENTATION OF CHRIST— THE LATE SERIES OF WORK OF THE DRAWINGS

Thoughts on death and knowledge of the finite nature of earthly existence, but also the hope of redemption, are directly interwoven with the last decades of Michelangelo's life. In his poems and letters, he gave the clearest expression to this sense of the proximity of death and loneliness, as he was increasingly tormented by a kidney disease. He was plunged into deep despair by the death of his close friend Vittoria Colonna, the

"What wonder is it if I, who when near the fire was destroyed and burned up by it, should now, when it has been extinguished outside of me, be tormented and consumed by it within, and little by little reduce myself to ashes?

In my burning state, I used to see so radiant the place which was the source of my heavy torment that the very sight of it made me happy, and death and anguish were to me feast days and sport.

But now that heaven has robbed me of the splendor of that great fire which set me on fire yet nourished me, I am an ember burning still but buried.

And if love does not grant me fresh wood to raise a flame, then not a single spark will be left of me, so quickly am I turning myself to ashes."

In his sonnet, Michelangelo laments the death of Vittoria Colonna in 1547.

marchioness of Pescara, who died on February 25, 1547 in Rome. Both his passionate admiration for this woman and his grief—he was "a long time in despair and as if out of his mind" about her death—were expressed in the form of a sonnet (see box) (Condivi).

The sense of abandonment continued to intensify for Michelangelo after he lost not only Vittoria Colonna but also his most important friends from the end of the 1540s. Thus, in November 1546 Luigi del Riccio died; he was a respected Florentine banker, whom Michelangelo is thought to have known since around 1533–34 and who not only attended to his business matters but also cared for him during his illnesses of 1544 and 1545–46. Michelangelo's loyal assistant Francesco Urbino, who had stood at his side for twenty-six years, died in January 1556, and in November 1555 his younger brother Gismondo died. After the death of his father and brothers, Michelangelo was now the only remaining member of his inner family circle. The letters from this period pay shocking testimony to Michelangelo's world-weariness and his yearning for death. To his nephew Lionardo, his brother Buonarroto's son, he wrote in December 1555 that Urbino's death had left him "so stricken and troubled that it would have been more easeful to die with him" and that since Urbino's death he had felt "lifeless myself." To Duke Cosimo I de' Medici, who wanted to persuade Michelangelo to return to Florence, he replied in May 1557 that he would only ever return to Florence "with my mind upon my repose with death, to which I seek to accustom myself day and night, that he may not treat me worse than other old men."

Michelangelo's preoccupation with death and his religious concern, his struggle with the mystery of redemption through Christ's sacrificial death, find expression in the last important work series of drawings on the theme of the Lamentation and the Crucifixion, including some folios produced for Vittoria

▷ **After Michelangelo**, *Pietà Drawing for Vittoria Colonna*, ca. 1540(?).
Black chalk, 11½ x 7½ in. (29.5 x 19.3 cm).
Isabella Gardner Stewart Museum, Boston, Massachusetts.

PAGES 204–205
Florentine Pietà (Bandini Pietà) (detail), ca. 1547–55.
Marble, 89 in. (226 cm) high.
Museo dell'Opera del Duomo, Florence.

Figure study for a Lamentation of Christ, 1530.
Black chalk, 11 x 10¼ in. (28.2 x 26.2 cm).
British Museum, London.

*"Relieved of a troublesome and heavy burden,
my dear Lord, and freed from the world, I
turn wearily to you, like a fragile boat passing
from a terrible storm to a pleasant calm.*

*The thorns and nails and both your palms,
together with your kind, humble, merciful face,
promise to the sinful soul the grace of deep
repentance and the hope of salvation.*

*May your holy eyes and pure ears not respond
with rigorous justice to my past life; may your
severe arm not stretch out toward it.*

*May your blood alone cleanse and remove my
sins; and may it more abound the older I am,
with ready help and with complete forgiveness."*

*Michelangelo's late sonnet is thought
to have been written in 1555 or later.*

Colonna. Thus he created "For love of this lady…a drawing of Jesus Christ on the Cross, not in the usual semblance of death, but alive, with His face upturned to the Father, and He seems to be saying, 'Eli, Eli.' Here we see that body not as an abandoned corpse falling, but as a living being, contorted and suffering in bitter torment" (Condivi).

He also created for Vittoria Colonna an unpreserved drawing of a *Pietà*, which Condivi describes in detail: "At this lady's request, he made a nude figure of Christ when He is taken from the Cross, which would fall as an abandoned corpse at the feet of His most holy mother, if it were not supported under the arms by two little angels. But she, seated beneath the Cross with a tearful and grieving countenance, raises both hands to heaven with open arms, with this utterance, which is inscribed on the stem of the Cross: *Non vi si pensa quanto sangue costa*" (Condivi). This inscription on the Cross, meaning "one would not think how much blood it costs" is a verse from Dante's "Paradise" in *The Divine Comedy*. A chalk drawing by Michelangelo that is now preserved in the Isabella Stewart Gardner Museum in Boston shows strong similarities with the above-mentioned *Pietà* drawing (ill. p.207). This work from ca. 1540–44 reveals the change in the treatment of the Lamentation theme, if we consider the *Pietà* of his youth in St. Peter's (ill. p.35), or even the earlier figure studies in which Michelangelo composed this subject (ill. p.208). Here nothing remains to be felt of the peaceful equilibrium in the disposition of the figures of mother and son. The composition is emphasized by Christ's

sunken body: he is no longer resting embedded in his mother's lap; vertical, with legs bent, he is placed between Mary's knees, his arms held by two angels. Christ appears abandoned in his deathly state; his mother is no longer turning toward him protectively: her countenance is upturned, and the gesture of the Madonna's arms raised high away from Christ reinforces the impression of Christ's abandonment.

After Vittoria Colonna's death, Michelangelo portrayed the crucified Christ in some further chalk and charcoal drawings (ill. p.209). In these drawings, Mary and other auxiliary figures, including Nicodemus and John, are grouped in various compositions at the sides of the dead Christ on the Cross. The folio preserved in Oxford is an impressive example of eloquent gestures in the auxiliary figures that convey grief and horror at Christ's suffering and death, as in the gesture of the figure on the right, which freezes statue-like in its pain, with hands placed on head in a helpless gesture. In research, the figure was long interpreted as Mary, with John as her counterpart; more

▷ Crucified Christ with two auxiliary figures (John and Mary?), ca. 1534–38.
Black chalk heightened with white, 11 x 9¼ in. (27.8 x 23.4 cm).
Ashmolean Museum, University of Oxford, England.

Cristofano dell'Altissimo, *Portrait of Michelangelo Buonarroti*, 1566, from the series of famous men in the corridor of the Uffizi Gallery.
Oil on canvas, 23½ x 17¼ in. (60 x 44 cm). Uffizi Gallery, Florence.

recently, the figures are seen possibly as representing soldiers (Zöllner et al.).

There is a surprising contrast in these drawings between the precision of the Cross drawn with the ruler and the extensive renunciation of anatomical details, including folios in which the bodily forms of the auxiliary figures appear almost abstract, only vaguely indicated, as if hidden behind a veil of fog—Christ's suffering and sacrificial death appear just like the iconographic transposition of an inner vision of Michelangelo's. Perhaps the most powerful message of the dialogue between mother and son are the late marble Pietà sculptures.

THE MARBLE PIETÀS

From around the early 1550s, Michelangelo created his last sculpted works, which are dedicated to the theme of the Lamentation of Christ. There are two groups of sculptures, all unfinished, which demonstrate a fundamental shift in the representation of Our Lady of Sorrows with the body of Christ taken down from the Cross. This can be impressively

observed from *Florentine Pietà* (ill. p.211), whose origination is predominantly established by research as between 1550 and 1555–57, but according to some also as early as the late 1540s. Vasari, who described the group as a work "a rare achievement in a single stone and truly inspired," and also Condivi, report that Michelangelo had intended the sculpture for his own grave, although this intention was never realized (Vasari).

For Condivi, what was unusual about the group was the way in which the figures are "perceived distinctly and the draperies of any one figure are not to be confused with those of the others" (Condivi). The figure of the man with the hood, who is holding the right arm of Christ's sunken body at the summit of the pyramidal group, is interpreted by some authors as Nicodemus—following Condivi—and by others as Joseph of Arimathea; both are mentioned in John's Gospel (John 7) in the entombment. The fact that—as is generally accepted—Michelangelo made a self-portrait in the figure's countenance could be seen as evidence of a reference to his own preoccupation with the theme. If we consider the story of Nicodemus, who only sought out Christ in the night, in secret, to talk with him about the eternal life, it seems an obvious supposition to interpret Michelangelo's self-portrait in the Nicodemus figure as a reference to the artist's sense of guilt at, like Nicodemus, not having revealed his own belief more clearly (John 3).

In his extensive study in 1960 of Michelangelo's final Pietà concepts, Alexander Perrig described *Florentine Pietà* as a "revision" of all the Pietà representations previously created by Michelangelo. In it the shift of emphasis in the relationship between the Virgin Mary and Christ is determined in favor of the latter; in contrast to the *Pietà* drawing discussed (ill. p.207) Mary turns here to her son with warmth, to which Condivi refers with "slips her breast, arms, and knee under His body." Christ, who no longer, as in the early Roman *Pietà*, rests embedded in his mother's lap, stands in the center of the composition. His dead body, portrayed in a complicated serpentinata-type movement, looking broken, is held by the other three figures. Thus, Mary supports her son, holding him with her left hand under the left armpit and stopping

Florentine Pietà (Bandini Pietà), ca. 1547–55.
Marble, 89 in. (226 cm) high.
Museo dell'Opera del Duomo, Florence.

Condivi gave a powerful description of the four-figure group chiseled from a marble block: "This is a group of four figures over life-size, consisting of a Christ deposed from the Cross, whose dead body is sustained by His mother, as she slips her breast, arms, and knee under His body in a remarkable pose. However, she is assisted from above by Nicodemus, who, erect and firm on his legs, with a display of vigorous strength supports the body under the arms; and from the left side she is assisted by one of the Marys, who, although visibly deeply grieved, nevertheless does not fail in the task to which the mother, in her extreme sorrow, is not equal. The released Christ falls with all His limbs slackened" (Condivi).

him from sinking down, while on the right Mary Magdalene supports the dead body of Christ. The actions and the emotional expressions of the auxiliary figures are retracted to the utmost; everything seems to be structured around the body of the Redeemer, the deathly state of the deceased (Perrig) from which all life force has ebbed away. On the faces of the auxiliary figures can be observed a muted suffering. In the figure of Nicodemus (Joseph of Arimathea) who towers over the group, the element of protection and inner participation is most clearly expressed.

Until around 1555, Michelangelo worked on the group, before he smashed it with a hammer. Like the exact time of the event, the reasons for Michelangelo's action have not been definitively explained to this day. Neither Vasari's anecdotally emphasized justification, which attributed the destruction to the pressure for completion that had issued from the assistant Francesco Urbino, nor Michelangelo's alleged dissatisfaction with the structure of the marble have emerged as irrefutable explanatory endeavors. Essentially the hammer blows struck the body of Christ: the left leg, the right lower arm, the right hand, the left elbow and lower arm, as well as the left part of the chest. The damage is still visible today: Part of Christ's left leg is missing, his left arm is broken over the elbow, and there are also visible fractures in his left chest and the fingers of Maria's left hand.

According to Vasari, Michelangelo left the smashed *Pietà* to Francesco Bandini, a Florentine banker exiled in Rome with whom Michelangelo had been friends since the days of the Florentine republic, which is why it is also known as *Bandini Pietà*. Bandini then wanted to have it completed by Michelangelo's pupil, the sculptor and architect Tiberio Calcagni (1532–65). Calcagni finished Mary Magdalene and wanted to retouch some other parts as well, such as replacing Christ's left leg—but his death in 1565 put an end to these plans. In 1664, the sculpture group was taken to Florence at the behest of the Grand Duke Cosimo III de' Medici, where it was installed first in San Lorenzo and finally in 1722 behind the high altar of Florence Cathedral. In 1933, it found its place there in a chapel of the north choir, until at the end of the 1960s it reached the cathedral museum.

It is thought that between 1550 and 1560 a further Pietà was created, the so-called *Pietà of Palestrina* (ill. p.213). On the basis that this work is not mentioned either by Vasari and Condivi or in the documents of the period, the attribution of this group of figures as the work of Michelangelo's own hand has been considered one of the most contentious questions in research. Standpoints ranged from the supposition that Michelangelo had merely hewn the group that was then executed by a

successor to the view that only the Mary Magdalene figure had been executed by Michelangelo's student Tiberio Calcagni. The vast Michelangelo volume recently edited by Frank Zöllner and others assigns the group definitely to the "circle" of Michelangelo (Zöllner).

We should also emphasize here the above-mentioned paper by Alexander Perrig, in which he defends the authenticity of *Pietà of Palestrina* essentially on the basis that it illustrates the "paradox of the events surrounding Christ," which the author understands as the central message that connects the late marble Pietàs: "In the hardness of the stone, the *living*

Michelangelo's circle, *Pietà of Palestrina*, ca. 1550–60. Marble, 99½ in. (253 cm) high. Galleria dell'Accademia, Florence.

The group that is carved into the fragment of a Roman architrave—traces of which can still be identified on the back—owes its name to its original installation site in the funeral chapel of Cardinal Antonio Barberini in the church of Santa Rosalia in Palestrina (Latium). In 1939, it was acquired by the Italian state and designated for installation in the Galleria dell'Accademia in Florence. On the group, designed for viewing only from the front, the imbalance between some of the individual proportions is immediately striking. Thus, for instance, the auxiliary figure of Mary Magdalene on Christ's left appears to have turned out too small, while Christ's right arm and the Virgin Mary's right hand, as she holds him under the armpit, appear strikingly large.

◁ *Florentine Pietà (Bandini Pietà)* (detail with the head of Mary Magdalene and the right hand of Christ), ca. 1547–55. Museo dell'Opera del Duomo, Florence.

213

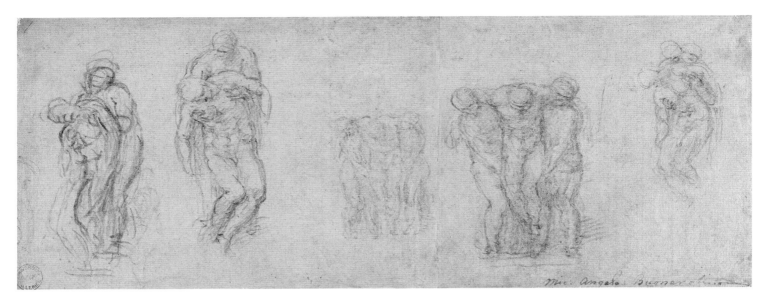

Studies for *Rondanini Pietà*, ca. 1552(?).
Black chalk, 4¼ x 11 in. (10.8 x 28.2 cm).
Ashmolean Museum, University of Oxford, England.

▷ *Rondanini Pietà*, unfinished final version, 1564.
Marble, 76¾ in. (195 cm) high.
Castello Sforzesco, Milan.

contradiction was to be overcome: to form Christ as the human being broken by death and *at the same time* to reveal in him the divine power that is capable of overcoming a person's own death; to represent the mother's all-surpassing pain and at the same time her 'knowledge' that overcomes her pain, namely that he whom she is already holding dead in her arms, despite his deathly state, is more powerful than she" (Perrig).

Perrig sees the resolution of this contradiction through its overcoming in art as Michelangelo's enduring motivation in his creative work, presupposing a perpetual conflict in the artist between the certainty of his belief and deep doubts about the illustration of his message. If we may not entirely accept Perrig's position on the question of authenticity, this conclusion nevertheless points to what may be a definitive explanation for the *non finito*, the unfinished quality, of the late Pietàs. Michelangelo's inherent doubt about his ability completely to transpose his central concern, the message of Christ's suffering and the notion of redemption, or overcome the "living contradiction" in the sculptural work, can thus be seen as a reason for his having left them as fragments.

In summer 1561 while it was still in progress, Michelangelo gave his last sculptural work, *Rondanini Pietà*, thought to have begun between 1550 and 1553, to his servant Antonio del Francese (ill. p.215). Vasari mentions the work, as does Michelangelo's friend Daniele da Volterra in two letters to Michelangelo's nephew Lionardo, and the estate catalog drawn up in Rome also presents the group as "another Christ statue in progress and a further figure standing over it, connected together, hewn and not completed" (Baldini). In 1652, the work was with a dealer in Rome, from where it may have gone directly to the Palazzo Rondanini, where it remained in the courtyard for over one hundred years, before coming into the possession of Count Sanseverino, from whom it was then acquired by the city of Milan in 1952 for 125 million lire and designated for the museum in Castello Sforzesco, where it is now preserved.

The version that can be seen today contains clearly discernible traces of a first version that Michelangelo had begun in the same block—such as the free-standing right arm-stump separated from the body of Christ and the originally different arrangement of the Virgin Mary's head. These enduring traces suggest an original conception that showed Christ being taken down from the Cross or the Entombment (Tolnay) with a muscularly formed body of Christ. This first version is thought to have occupied Michelangelo until 1553. In the second version that incorporated the first, on which he worked from 1554 until 1564, the final days before his death, Michelangelo turned the subject into a *Pietà*. In this connection, reference should be made to the cleaning works on the sculpture that had already been prepared in 1998 through extensive investigations. Like *David* (ill. p.43), *Rondanini Pietà* underwent a cleaning process that used strips of Japanese rice paper dipped in distilled water. One of the discoveries that emerged from the restoration measures concluded in 2004 in Milan was that a head of Christ found in the 1950s in Rome, which had been attributed since 1973 to the first version of *Rondanini Pietà* (the so-called Borghese fragment), was recognized as definitely not belonging to the block following petrographic investigations of the marble (Bicci).

In *Rondanini Pietà*, with its aura of mystery that is still emphasized by art criticism today, the connection between mother and son undergoes a final intensification: the figures appear to be literally intertwined, and the laws of logic and gravity to be suspended. Mother and son appear to be

completely concentrated on themselves together; no auxiliary figures bring any activity into what is taking place. The mother, who is standing on a cliff, is certainly supporting the dead son's body, but this only occurs in outline. There is no longer any indication of the enduring power of the Virgin Mary in *Florentine Pietà*. Perrig understands the Virgin Mary's nestling also as a natural "response" to the body leaning against her, the gesture of her arm laid around the son's shoulder and chest as expressing the fact that she has the dead one with her. The treatment of the surfaces that reveals the artist's creative process and the renunciation of a perfect elaboration of anatomical forms—everything serves the intensification of emotional expression that takes precedence over the bodily forms. In this respect, the sculpture already prefigures the design principles of the sculptural works of the twentieth century. Thus, for instance, William E. Wallace associates the abstract forms of *Rondanini Pietà* with the bird-sculptures of Constantin Brancusi.

Rondanini Pietà, Michelangelo's final artistic message, also marks the culmination of his increased spirituality and his religious feeling in the late creative years—an enduring message in which mother and son, united in suffering, point the viewer a way to understanding the sacrificial death of Jesus Christ. On February 12, 1564, Michelangelo was still working on *Rondanini Pietà*; a few days later, on February 18, he died after a "slow fever" at the age of eighty-nine years (Vasari). His nephew Lionardo did not reach his death bed in Rome in time, but Michelangelo did not die alone. According to the sources, in addition to his doctor Federigo Donati, his companions Daniele da Volterra and Tommaso de' Cavalieri, as well as his servant Antonio del Francese, were with him. In accordance with the wish he expressed on his death bed, he was taken to Florence, a trip that took place in secret. Sewn into a linen cloth, "in a bale, disguised as a piece of merchandise," on March 11, 1564, he made the final journey to his native city, where the formal exequies took place on July 14 in San Lorenzo and he was interred in the church of Santa Croce with many Florentine citizens in attendance. Until 1568, the sculptors Battista Lorenzi and Valerio Cioli were occupied with the execution of his tomb, which had been designed by Vasari (ill. p.216).

Before his death, Michelangelo had burned many more drawings, sketches, and cartoons to prevent anyone seeing, according to Vasari, "the labors he endured and the ways he tested his genius, and lest he should appear less than perfect." The inventory of his possessions made after his death by the notary Roberto Ubaldini testifies to the artist's modest, truly Spartan, way of life. He lived till the end in Rome in almost

◁ Michelangelo's tomb in Santa Croce, designed by Giorgio Vasari, sculptures by Valeria Cioli, Battista Lorenzi, Giovanni dell'Opera, 1564–75. Marble. Santa Croce, Florence.

> "Lionardo,
> I had your last letter with twelve
> most excellent and delicious
> marzolini cheeses, for which
> I thank you.
> I'm delighted at your well-being;
> the same is true of me. Having
> received several letters of yours
> recently and not having replied,
> I have omitted to do so, because
> I can't use my hand to write; therefore
> from now on I'll get others to write and
> I'll sign. I think that's all.
> From Rome on the 28th Day of
> December 1563."
>
> *Michelangelo's last letter, written to his nephew Lionardo seven weeks before his death.*

impoverished circumstances in his modest house in Macello dei Corvi, near Trajan's Forum—an estate that reflects none of the recognition and high regard that was accorded Michelangelo during his life. As Vasari described it, "As we have seen, Julius II, Leo X, Clement VII, Paul III, Julius III, Paul IV, and Pius IV, all these supreme pontiffs, wanted to have him near them at all times; as also, as we know, did Suleiman, emperor of the Turks, Francis of Valois, king of France, the Emperor Charles V, the Signoria of Venice, and lastly, as I related, Duke Cosimo de' Medici, all of whom made him very honorable offers, simply to avail themselves of his great talents. This happens only to men of tremendous worth, like Michelangelo, who, as was clearly recognized, achieved in the three arts a perfect mastery that God has granted no other person, in the ancient or modern world, in all the years that the sun has been spinning round the world" (Vasari).

STARTLING MODERNITY...

The quasi-Expressionist tendencies of the late *Rondanini Pietà* mark only one peak in Michelangelo's creative work, which to many anticipates the developments in art of later centuries. The astounding modernity of his conception of art is attested by a conversation recorded by the Portuguese painter and architect Francisco de Hollanda (1517–84) in which Michelangelo made the following comment about art and artists: "For if we rightly consider everything that we do in this life, we will find that everyone in the world, without knowing it, paints: by the creation and production of new forms and figures, by clothing and dress; by filling space with buildings and houses that are similar to paintings; in the cultivation of the earth's fields and land in long furrows…and finally in dying and being buried, in short—in each and everything that we do" (Erpel). Four centuries later, Joseph Beuys would formulate his thoughts about artistic creativity in which all human beings could participate.

In Michelangelo the human being we also encounter a personality whose feeling reveals astonishing proximities to the states of consciousness of the modern human being. He was modern in his suffering from reality, as well as being at the mercy of the patrons, for which the tragedy of the tomb for Pope Julius II tormented him for forty years, became poignantly symbolic—a suffering that also manifested itself in the consciousness of solitude that characterized his mature creative period. He was modern also in his pragmatism, which not infrequently led him to dictate to his biographers Vasari and Condivi a "corrected" picture of the actual events as they wrote—in self-defense and self-protection in the difficult political times. Michelangelo was also modern in his enduring concern for his family, which he did not only understand lovingly: he interfered forcefully in family matters from Rome, wrathfully reprimanding his younger brother Giovansimone, a real idler, who was threatening their father, in a letter: "Now I'm certain that you are not my brother.… On the contrary, you are a brute, and as a brute I shall treat you." By contrast, there is some moving advice from the nearly seventy-four-year-old man to his favorite nephew, Lionardo, in relation to marriage, not of course without warning him against women: "It's up to you to marry or not to marry, or rather to choose one girl rather than another, provided she is of noble family and well brought up and rather without a dowry than with a large one."

We encounter a person who preferred solitude to diversion, who, miserly toward himself, lived to the end in impoverished conditions in his Roman flat, but who also, as is frequently attested in his letters by instructions to his family to buy this or that piece of land, was constantly preoccupied with increasing his private means. Thus, Antonio Forcellino mentions that at Michelangelo's death a "chest full of gold pieces" hidden under his bed came to light "that would have been enough to acquire the entire Pitti Palace" (Forcellino). He was someone who dismissed collaborators on the spot if they did not meet his requirements, but who equally was plunged into deep grief by the loss of his close assistant Francesco Urbino who had accompanied him for twenty-six years, a grief that even destroyed his will to live. He was a person whose curtness and irascible character is emphasized by his biographers, whose *terribilità* instilled fear and respect alike in his contemporaries, but whose poems testify to a deep sensibility, which the Michelangelo translator Michael Engelhard understands to be a language of the most personal experience of existence, also discerning in his writing an absolutely startling modernity. As a person and an artist, he suffered from the irreconcilability of ideal and reality, to which the sculptures he left in a fragmentary state give testimony.

Michelangelo's human nature is as complex as his artistry, if also much more inherently contradictory. Any preoccupation with his personality and extensive work can only be an approximation that leaves many questions open, as it was expressed by Fritz Erpel in his subtle afterword to the German edition of Condivi's *Life of Michelangelo*: "There are open questions to this day. Questions that in the meantime do nothing to detract from the simple truth toward which Condivi pointed with this writing: that our age will remain indebted to Michelangelo for the abundance of light that proceeds from the works and from the man himself. Michelangelo's universal picture of the human being dispensed with any yardstick or frontier; it remained elevated as a shining moment in humanity."

Emilio Santarelli, *Statue of Michelangelo*, 1840–45, from the series of 28 statues of famous men on the portico of the Uffizi Gallery, Florence.

MICHELANG. BUONARROTI

BIBLIOGRAPHY

Addington Symonds, J.: *The Life of Michelangelo Buonarroti*, New York 1928

Baldini, Umberto: *Das bildhauerische Gesamtwerk von Michelangelo*, Milan 1973

Beck, J.: *Three Worlds of Michelangelo*, New York and London 1999

Benkard, Ernst: *Michelangelos Madonna an der Treppe*, Berlin 1933

Bicci, Antonella: *Risplende la Pietà Rondanini*, 06.16.2004 (www.exibart.com, Link "restauri")

Bredekamp, Horst: *Sankt Peter in Rom und das Prinzip der produktiven Zerstörung*, Berlin 2000

Burckhardt, Jacob: *The Civilization of the Renaissance in Italy*, New York 2002

Condivi, Ascanio: *The Life of Michelangelo*, trans. Alice Sedgwick, ed. Hellmut Wohl, Baton Rouge LA 1976

Dante Aleghieri: *The Divine Comedy*, trans. Mark Musa, London 1984

F. Baumgart and B. Biagetti: "Die Fresken des Michelangelo," L. Sabbatini and F. Zuccari in *Der Cappella Paolina im Vatikan*, Introduction Vatican 1934

Echinger-Maurach, Claudia: *Studien zu Michelangelos Juliusgrabmal*, Hildesheim, Zurich, New York 1991

Echinger-Maurach, Claudia: "Gli occhi fissi nella somma bellezza del Figliuolo—Michelangelo im Wettstreit mit Leonardos Madonnenconcetti der zweiten Florentiner Periode," in: Michael Rohlmann und Axel Thielmann (ed.): *Michelangelo. Neue Beiträge*, Munich, Berlin 2000

Eliot, Alexander: "Was wird davon übrig bleiben?" in: *Art*, 11 1987, pp. 28–44 and 130

Erpel, Fritz (ed.): *Ich—Michelangelo. Briefe, Dichtungen und Gespräche in einer Auswahl*, Berlin 1966

Goethe, Johann Wolfgang von: *Italian Journey*, trans. W. H. Auden, ed. Elizabeth Mayer, London 1992

Justi, Carl: *Michelangelo. Neue Beiträge zur Erklärung seiner Werke*, Berlin 1909

Kupper, Daniel: *Michelangelo*, Hamburg 2004

Landucci, L. A.: *Florentine Diary*, trans. Alice de Rosen Jervis, London 1927

Longhi, Roberto: *Kurze, aber wahre Geschichte der italienischen Malerie*, Cologne 1996

Michelangelo: *The Letters*, 2 vols., trans. and ed. E. H. Ramsden, Stanford 1963

Michelangelo: *The Poems*, trans. Christopher Ryan, London 1996

Panofsky, Erwin: *Tomb Sculpture: Four Lectures on its Changing Aspects from Ancient Egypt to Bernini*, trans. H. W. Janson, New York 1992

Partridge, Loren: *The Art of the Renaissance in Rome 1400–1600*, Upper Saddle River NJ 2005

Perrig, Alexander: *Michelangelos letzte Pietà-Idee*, Berne 1960

Schwedes, Kerstin: "Michelangelos, *Römische Pietà*," in: Michael Rohlmann *op. cit.*

Stützer, Herbert Alexander: *Die Italienische Renaissance*, Cologne 1986

Tolnay, Charles de: *The Sistine Ceiling*, Princeton 1945

Tolnay, Charles de: *The Youth of Michelangelo*, Princeton 1947

Vasari, Giorgio: "Leonardo da Vinci, Raphael, and Michelangelo," in: *Lives of the Artists*, trans. Jonathan Foster, ed. Marilyn Aronberg Lavin, New York 2005

Vecchi, Pierluigi de (ed.): *Michelangelo*, Cologne 1991

Vecchi, Pierluigi de (ed.): *The Sistine Chapel: A Glorious Restoration*, New York 1994

Wallace, William E.: *Michelangelo: The Complete Sculpture, Painting, Architecture*, Westport CT 1998

Walter, Ingeborg: *Der Prächtige. Lorenzo de'Medici und seine Zeit*, Munich 2003

Wittkower, Rudolf: *Allegory and the Migration of Symbols*, London 1977

PICTURE CREDITS

© akg images, Berlin: 57, 71 left, rear fold-out: 4 center top, 5 center, 5 right — 2, 4, 9, 16 right, 46 left, 71 right, 80, 81, 96 top, 97, 98–99, 100–101, 104–105, 111, 112, 113, 114, 115, 116 top, 117, 118–9, 120, 121, 186–7, 194, 198, jacket, inside fold-out: 2, rear fold-out: 3 center, 6 top right (Erich Lessing) — 6–7, 18–19, 21, 26, 40–41, 62, 65–6, 69, 73, 75, 76, 87, 130 right bottom, 140, 147, 148 top, 152, 153, 204–205, 210, 211, 217, rear fold-out: 3 right bottom (Rabatti – Domingie) — 48 left, 203, 214 left, 214 right (Nimatallah) — 67, 74, 78–9, 149 top, 149 bottom, 212 (Andrea Jemolo) — 219 (Gérard Degeorge) — rear fold-out: 6 M. (Cameraphoto) — rear fold-out: 6 bottom right (Hervé Champollion)

© akg images/Electa: 162–3, 166–7

© Alinari/Bridgeman Berlin: 77

© Ashmolean Museum, University of Oxford, UK/Bridgeman Berlin: 51, 154, 209, 214

© Bridgeman Berlin: 15 right, 20, 34 left, 34 right, 46 right, 48 left, 49 top, 56 left, 66, 127, 145, 191, 192

© British Museum, London/Bridgeman Berlin: 86, 96 bottom, 155, 164, 208 top, inside fold-out 8

© Collection of the Earl of Leicester, Holkham Hall, Norfolk/Bridgeman Berlin: 49 bottom

© Corbis, Düsseldorf: rear fold-out: 4 right

© Giraudon/The Bridgeman Art Library: 182 left

© Haarlem, Teylers Museum: 141 bottom

© Hervé Champollion/akg images, Berlin: 197, 200 bottom

© Isabella Stewart Gardner Museum, Boston (MA)/Bridgeman Berlin: 207

© Musée Condé, Chantilly/Bridgeman Berlin: 116 bottom

© Photo Opera Metropolitana Siena/Scala, Florence: 60, 61
The Royal Collection © 2007, Her Majesty Queen Elizabeth II: 156

© Scala, Florence: 8, 13 top, 13 bottom, 14, 25, 33, 35, 36, 38, 39, 54, 59, 63, 70, 89, 122, 126, 130 bottom left, 131, 142 right top, 146 bottom, 148 bottom, 151 top, 151 bottom, 157, 160, 162 top left, 178, 179, 180, 181, 183, 184, 189, 193, 195, 196, 199, 200 top, 201, 202, rear fold-out: 1, 3 left, 4 left, 6 left — 10–11 (Courtesy of Servizio Musei Comunali) — 12, 16 left 19 top, 22–3, 24, 27, 32, 42, 43, 44,

45, 47, 50, 52–3, 55, 56 right, 58, 124–5, 128, 129, 132 left top, 132–3, 133 right, 134, 135, 136 bottom left, 136–7, 138 bottom left, 138 top right, 139, 141 top, 142 top left, 143, 144, 146 top, 150, 185, 190 top, 190 bottom, 213, rear fold-out: 3 right top, 8 (Courtesy of the Ministero Beni e Att. Culturali) — 28 left, 30, 31 (Luciano Romano)

© Scala, Florence/Fondo Edifici di Culto – Min. dell'Interno: 15 left, 17 left, 28 left, 29, 182 right, rear fold-out: 5 left

© Vatican Museums, Photographic Archives of the Vatican Museums: 88–9, 158–9, 161, 165, 168–9, 170–71, 174, 175, 176–7 — 7, 82–3, 85, 90–91, 92–3, 94–5, 102–103, 106–107, 108 top, 108 bottom, 109, 110, 123, 172–3, rear fold-out: 2–7 (A. Bracchetti/P. Zigrossi)— inside fold-out: Gesamtansicht (Bracchetti/ Zigrossi/Giordano)

Ill. p.2
Giuliano Bugiardini *Portrait of Michelangelo Buonarroti with Turban,* ca. 1522
Oil on wood, 19¼ x 14¼ in. (49 x 36.4 cm)
Musée du Louvre, Paris

Ill. p.4
Libyan Sibyl, 1511–12
Fresco, 157½ x 149½ in. (400 x 380 cm)
Vatican, Sistine Chapel, Rome

Rear fold-out:
Ill. p.1
Jacopino del Conte *Portrait of Michelangelo,* ca. 1535.
Oil on canvas, 38¾ x 26¾ in. (98.5 x 68 cm)
Casa Buonarroti, Florence

Ill. pp.2–7
The Last Judgment, 1536–41, detail of the lower left lunette with angels carrying the Golgotha Cross

Ill. p.8
David, 1501–04, detail of the head
Galleria dell'Accademia, Florence

ACKNOWLEDGMENT
Many thanks go to Lioba Waleczek and Michael Konze for their support and commitment on this project and Helga Berger for her careful reading of the manuscript.

Yvonne Paris, January 2008

This is a Parragon Publishing Book

This edition published in 2009

Parragon Publishing
Queen Street House
4 Queen Street
Bath BA1 1HE, UK

Copyright © Parragon Books Ltd 2009

ISBN 978-1-4075-4271-3

Printed in China

German edition created and produced by:
Lioba Waleczek, Michael Konze, Cologne
Design: Elisabeth Hardenbicker, Cologne
Reproduction: farbo prepress, Cologne

US edition produced by:
Cambridge Publishing Management Ltd
Project editor: Penny Isaac
Translation: Sophie Leighton
Copy editor: Nina Hnatov
Typesetter: Julie Crane
Proofreader: Karolin Thomas

	Biography	Culture	History

Biography

1475 Michelangelo Buonarroti is born on March 6, the second son of Ludovico di Buonarroti Simoni and Francesca di Neri. On March 8, he is baptized in the church of San Giovanni. In April the family returns to Florence, with the ending of his father's term of office as *Podestà* (chief magistrate). Three more brothers are born between 1477 and 1481.

1481 On December 6, his mother Francesca dies.

1485 Michelangelo begins drawing, encouraged by his friend Francesco Granacci. His father marries Lucrezia degli Ubaldini.

1488 Michelangelo's father agrees to a training contract for his son at the workshop of the Florentine artists, brothers Davide and Domenico Ghirlandaio.

Apollonius, *Belvedere Torso*, ca. 40 BC. Marble, 62½ in. (159 cm) high. Vatican, Museo Pio-Clementino, Sala delle Muse, Rome.

1489 Michelangelo ends the training early. Studies in the sculpture garden of Lorenzo de' Medici. Influenced by the circle of humanists at Lorenzo's court around Angelo Poliziano and Marsilio Ficino.

1491 Produces first two sculptural works: *Madonna of the Steps* and, in 1492, *Battle of the Centaurs*.

1492 After the death of his patron Lorenzo de' Medici, Michelangelo returns to his father. With permission from the prior of San Spirito in Florence he carries out anatomical studies using corpses.

1494 Political unrest in Florence and expulsion of Piero II de' Medici. Michelangelo flees to Bologna, where he produces the sculptures of *St. Proculus*, *St. Petronius*, and an angel candelabrum for the sarcophagus of St. Dominic.

1495 Return to Florence, where he creates a small *John the Baptist* and a sleeping *Cupid* for Pierfrancesco de' Medici, to be sold to Cardinal Riario in Rome.

1496 Cardinal Raffaele Riario invites him to Rome. Under his commission, Michelangelo produces *Drunken Bacchus*.

1497 Commission for the *Pietà* of St. Peter's (completed 1499). Travels to Carrara to choose marble.

1501 In June, Michelangelo receives the commission for fifteen statues for the Piccolomini altar in Siena Cathedral. In August, the Florentine wool-weavers guild commissions him for the marble statue of *David*. Receives commission for *Bruges Madonna*.

Culture

1475 Fresco painting of *Scenes from the Lives of Moses and Christ* in the Sistine Chapel by leading Italian painters such as Botticelli, Ghirlandaio, Perugino, and Signorelli. Pope Sixtus IV founds the Vatican Library.

1481 Filippino Lippi begins the Peter frescoes in the Brancacci Chapel of Santa Maria del Carmine. Michael Pacher completes the high altar in St. Wolfgang (Salzkammergut).

1488 Death of Andrea del Verrocchio, Italian sculptor and painter, who created his bronze statue of *David* in 1475.

1490 Domenico Ghirlandaio, Michelangelo's tutor, completes the fresco cycle with *Scenes from the Lives of Mary and John the Baptist* in Santa Maria Novella, Florence.

1492 The first globe, made by Martin Behaim, appears in Nuremberg. Death of Piero della Francesca, a late Gothic painter from Umbria.

1494 Albrecht Dürer makes his first journey to Italy, staying in Venice. The first textbook of arithmetic and algebra appears, Luca Pacioli's *Summa de Arithmetica*.

1495 Syphilis spreads from Naples as an epidemic throughout Europe.

1496 Raphael becomes a pupil of Perugino, who had collaborated on the fresco painting of the Sistine Chapel until circa 1482.

1497 Leonardo da Vinci completes the fresco of *The Last Supper* in the convent of Santa Maria delle Grazie, Milan.

1498 Albrecht Dürer paints his *Self-Portrait* and publishes a wood-engraving series, *Apocalypse*.

Albrecht Dürer, *Self-Portrait*, 1498. Oil on wood, 20½ x 16¼ in. (52 x 41 cm). Prado, Madrid.

1499 Luca Signorelli begins his major work, the frescoes in the Brizius Chapel in Orvieto Cathedral.

1501 Giovanni Bellini begins his famous portrait, *The Doge Leonardo Loredan* (until 1505).

1502 Donato Bramante's templet in the San Pietro monastery in Montorio (Rome) marks a high point of Renaissance architecture. Jacopo Sannarazo's pastoral poem "Arcadia" is a landmark for European literature. Erasmus of Rotterdam's *Handbook of the Christian Soldier*, which criticizes the Church, appears in Latin.

History

1475 Birth of Giovanni de' Medici, son of Lorenzo the Magnificent, later Pope Leo X.

Ottavio Giovannozzi, *Bust of Lorenzo the Magnificent*, 1825. Uffizi Gallery, Florence.

1478 Murder of Giuliano de' Medici.

1481 In Spain, the Inquisition is instigated.

1484 The Dominican monk Girolamo Savonarola comes to Florence and preaches the reform of religious and secular life.

1488 The Portuguese seafarer Bartolomeo Diaz sails around the southernmost point of Africa.

1492 Death of Lorenzo the Magnificent. Rodrigo Borgia becomes Pope Alexander VI (1492–1503). Christopher Columbus discovers America.

1494 Ludovico Sforza becomes Duke of Milan. After the fall of the Medici, Florence is ruled by Savonarola.

1495 Conquest of Naples by Charles V.

1496 Philip I's marriage to the Infanta Juana brings the Spanish crown to the House of Habsburg.

1497 Pope Alexander VI excommunicates Savonarola. The Florentine seafarer Amerigo Vespucci writes his account of his journeys to South America and Honduras.

1498 On May 23, Savonarola is hanged in Florence and burned as a heretic. Vasco da Gama discovers the sea route to India.

Unknown artist, *Execution of Savonarola on the Piazza della Signoria*. Oil on wood, 39¾ x 46 in. (101 x 117 cm). Museo di San Marco dell'Angelico, Florence.

1499 Conquest of the dukedom of Milan by the French King Louis XII. Vasco da Gama returns to Portugal and is made "Admiral of the Indian Seas" and a duke.

Biography	Culture	History

Biography

1502 — Commission from the Florentine government for a bronze *David* for Marshal Pierre de Rohan.

1503 — Commission for statues of the twelve apostles for Santa Maria del Fiore in Florence. Michelangelo executes only the *St. Matthew* statue.

Donatello, *Judith and Holofernes*, ca. 1454. Bronze, 93 in. (236 cm) high. Palazzo Vecchio, Florence.

1504 — Michelangelo's *David* is placed in front of the Palazzo della Signoria in Florence. He is commissioned by Piero Soderini to paint the fresco of *The Battle of Cascina* in the Great Hall of the Palazzo Vecchio, for which he prepares a cartoon. Work on the marble tondo of *Pitti Madonna*. Under commission from the merchant Agnolo Doni, he paints *Doni Tondo*.

1505 — Michelangelo is called to Rome by Pope Julius II, who commissions him for the Julius tomb. Visit to Carrara to choose the marble. Taddeo Taddei orders the *Taddei Tondo*.

1506 — Michelangelo tries to obtain funds for further work on the Julius tomb. Refused by the pope, he leaves Rome in a fit of rage.

1507 — After the reconciliation with Julius II, a visit to Bologna, where the bronze statue of Julius II is cast.

1508 — Installation of completed bronze statue over the façade of San Petronio (destroyed 1511). At end of March, he is commissioned by the pope to paint the Sistine Chapel ceiling.

1510 — Completion of the first half of the Sistine ceiling. Death of his brother Lionardo.

1512 — On October 31, the vault frescoes in the Sistine Chapel are officially inaugurated.

1513 — After the death of Pope Julius II, a second contract is agreed to with his heirs for the Julius tomb. The number of statues is reduced from forty-eight to twenty. Work on the figures of *Bound Captive* and *Dying Captive*. Begins work on the figure of *Moses* for the Julius tomb.

1516 — Third version of the contract for the Julius tomb. The Medici Pope Leo X commissions Michelangelo for the façade of San Lorenzo in Florence, the family church of the Medici (contract annulled 1520).

1517 — Michelangelo travels to the quarries of Seravezza to obtain the marble for San Lorenzo, but transportation of the vast blocks fails.

Culture

1503 Leonardo da Vinci receives the commission for the wall painting of *The Battle of Anghiari* in the Palazzo Vecchio, in Florence, which has only been preserved through copies. Parmigianino, a leading Mannerist painter, is born.

Leonardo da Vinci, *Virgin and Child with St. Anne*, 1502–13. Oil on wood, 66½ x 51¼ in. (169 x 130 cm). Louvre, Paris.

1505 Raphael paints the portraits of the merchant Agnolo Doni and his wife Maddelena (Florence, Palazzo Pitti). Donato Bramante designs the Cortile del Belvedere in the Vatican.

1506 The foundation stone is laid for the new construction of St. Peter's in Rome according to Bramante's plan. Discovery of the *Laocoön Group* on the Esquiline Hill in Rome. Leonardo completes the *Mona Lisa*.

1507 Death of Cesare Borgia, the archetypical power figure of the Renaissance (model for Machiavelli's *The Prince*). The name "America" appears for the first time on a world map by Matthias Ringmann and Martin Waldseemüller.

1508 Raphael begins to paint the papal apartments with the frescoes in the Stanza della Segnatura, *The School of Athens*.

1512 Raphael's portrait of Julius II becomes the prototype of the papal portrait of the Renaissance. In the *Commentariolus*, Copernicus outlines his heliocentric world view.

1515 Machiavelli publishes his major work, *The Prince*.

1517 The Florentine painter Andrea del Sarto paints his *Madonna of the Harpies*.

1518 Titian's altar picture, *Assumption of the Virgin*, for Santa Maria Gloriosa dei Frari, Venice, is completed.

Raphael, *Sistine Madonna*, 1513–14. Oil on canvas, 100¾ x 77¼ in. (256 x 196 cm). Gemäldegalerie Alte Meister, Dresden.

1519 Leonardo da Vinci dies on May 2 in the castle of Clos Lucé near Amboise, France where he had been living for the last 3 years.

1520 Luther publishes his three great Reformation works: *Address to the Nobility of the German Nation*, *On Christian Liberty*, and *On the Babylonish Captivity of the Church*. Raphael dies in Rome.

History

1501 Louis XII of France and Ferdinand of Aragon conquer the kingdom of Naples. Piero Soderini becomes *Gonfaloniere* of Florence.

1503 Giuliano della Rovere holds office as Pope Julius II until 1513. Founding of the Benedictine Order.

1504 In the Treaty of Blois, Louis XII recognizes that Naples has lost its independence to Spain. Beginning of the two-hundred-year Spanish-Habsburg rule in Southern Italy.

1507 Cesare Borgia, son of Pope Alexander VI, as a soldier in the service of his brother-in-law, is murdered on March 12 during the siege of Viana.

1508 Maximilian of Habsburg accepts the imperial title in the Cathedral of Trent and forms the League of Cambrai against Venice with France, Spain, and the pope.

1510 Pope Julius forms a "Sacred League" against France.

1515 The Medici return to power in Florence. Florence becomes a dukedom.

1513 Giovanni de' Medici becomes pope (Leo X, until 1521). Vasco Núñez de Balboa crosses the Isthmus of Panama and discovers the Pacific.

1515 In the battle of Marignano against the pope and the emperor, Francis I gains Milan and Genoa.

After a failed mutiny, Ferdinand de Magellan's crew swears the oath of loyalty to the captain.

1518 Martin Luther is interrogated in Augsburg by the papal legate Cardinal Cajetan. The elector of Saxony, Frederick the Wise, refuses to send Martin Luther to Rome.

1519 The Portuguese Ferdinand de Magellan is first to sail round the world and discovers the strait that is named after him. Hernán Cortéz conquers Mexico.

1520 Charles V is crowned emperor of the German nation of the Holy Roman Empire.

1521 Martin Luther is excommunicated. Pope Leo X dies, and is succeeded by

MICHELANGELO AND HIS TIME

Biography	Culture	History

Biography

1541 Inauguration of *The Last Judgment* on October 31.

1542 Final version of the contract for the Julius tomb. Executes the figures of *Leah* and *Rachel*; completes *Moses*. Work begins on the frescoes for the Pauline Chapel (1542–45).

1545 Completion of the Julius tomb in San Pietro in Vincoli. Ascanio Condivi becomes his student.

1546 Beginning of *The Crucifixion of Peter* in the Pauline Chapel (1546–50). Commission for the façade and inner courtyard of the Farnese Palace. In March, Michelangelo becomes a citizen of Rome.

Façade of the Farnese Palace, Rome, begun in 1514 by Antonio Sangallo the Younger, continued by Michelangelo 1546–49

1547 After the death of Sangallo the Younger, Michelangelo is appointed chief architect of St. Peter's. In February, death of Vittoria Colonna.

1550 Completion of the frescoes in the Pauline Chapel. Begins work on *Florentine Pietà* that Michelangelo intends for his own tomb. Vasari publishes the first edition of his *Lives of the Artists*, including the biography of Michelangelo.

1552 Thought to be the first version of *Rondanini Pietà*.

1555 Paul IV commissions Michelangelo for the cupola of St. Peter's. As the Inquisition gathers force, *The Last Judgment* is branded obscene.

1556 Death of his assistant Francesco di Bernardo dell' Amadore da Castelduranté, named Urbino.

1557 Michelangelo destroys *Bandini Pietà*.

1561 Execution of the plans for the Porta Pia and the conversion of Diocletian's Roman thermal baths in the church of Santa Maria degli Angeli.

1563 Death of Cesare Bettini on the building site of St. Peter's. Pope Pius IV orders an investigation that finds in Michelangelo's favor.

1564 On February 18, Michelangelo dies in Rome. In accordance with his last testament, his body is taken to Florence, where the burial ceremony takes place in San Lorenzo. In the wake of the Council of Trent, the private body parts in *The Last Judgment* are painted over.

Culture

1547 Tintoretto (Jacopo Robusti) paints *The Last Supper* in San Marcuola (Venice). Death of Sebastiono del Piombo, whose art was influenced by Michelangelo.

Villa Poiana, built by Andrea Palladio, 1548/49–1563

1548 Titian paints Emperor Charles V in Augsburg seated (Alte Pinakotek, Munich) and on horseback (Prado, Madrid).

1550 Cardinal Ippolito d'Este has the Villa d'Este built by Pirro Ligorio near Tivoli, with a park and fountains.

1552 The Englishman Edward Watton publishes his *De differentiis animalium*, a zoological text regarded as a precursor of Linnaeus' work.

1553 Ludovico Dolce publishes his translation of Ovid's *Metamorphoses*. The death of Lucas Cranach the Elder, court painter in Wittenberg since 1505.

1556 Death of Pietro Aretino, Italian writer and satirist, and of Ignatius Loyola. Birth of Carlo Maderno, Italian master builder who later completes the façade of the new St. Peter's.

1557 Founding of the Accademia di San Luca (art academy) in Rome.

1558 Giambattista della Porta publishes his *Magia Naturalis*.

1559 The first Catholic *Index librorum prohibitorum* (list of prohibited books) is published. The Anglican state church finally predominates over Catholicism in England.

1560 Giorgio Vasari supervises the building of the Uffizi Palace in Florence under commission from Duke Cosimo I. Lifting of the prohibition on the dissection of corpses in force since 1530.

1563 Paolo Veronese, one of the principal masters of Venetian painting, completes his famous painting, *The Wedding at Cana*.

1564 Giacomo da Vignola becomes construction supervisor of St. Peter's. Birth of William Shakespeare (in Stratford-upon-Avon) and Galileo Galilei (Italian scientist).

History

1547 King Francis I of France dies; he is succeeded by Henri II. A rift between Charles V and Pope Paul III. Coronation of the Tsar Ivan IV, named "the Terrible."

1549 Giovanni Maria Ciocchi del Monte is elected as Pope Julius III (1549–55).

1553 Mary I, the Catholic, succeeds Edward VI to the English throne (until 1558). Bloody persecution of Protestants in England.

1555 Pope Julius III dies. Marcellus II succeeds (for three weeks), then Paul IV (until 1559). Religious Peace of Augsburg: legal recognition of the Lutheran creed.

Peter Paul Rubens, *Allegorical Painting of Emperor Charles V as Ruler of the World*, ca. 1604. Residenzgalerie, Salzburg.

1556 In January Charles V passes Aragon, Sicily, and the "new India," to his son Philip II of Castile. His brother Ferdinand becomes Holy Roman Emperor.

1558 Charles V dies. Elizabeth I, daughter of Henry VIII and Anne Boleyn, is recognized by Parliament as Queen of England.

1559 Pius IV succeeds Paul IV to the papal throne (until 1565). The peace treaty of Le Cateau–Cambrésis on April 8 ends the battles between France under Henri II and Philip II of Spain for hegemony in Europe (Italian wars) and confirms the supremacy of the Habsburgs in Italy. First burnings of heretics in Seville and Valladolid.

1560 Catherine de' Medici, widow of Henri II, takes over the regency in France.

1562 Beginning of the Huguenot wars in France. The third Council of Trent establishes the Catholic creed and strengthens the pope's position.

1564 Ferdinand I, Holy Roman Emperor, dies and is succeeded by Maximilian II. The gulf between Catholicism and Protestantism widens.

Germain Pilon, double tomb of Henri II and Catherine de' Medici, 1583. Cathedral of Saint-Denis, Paris.

Biography

1519 Probable start of work on *Victor* figure for the Julius tomb. Work on the four *Boboli Slaves*. Commission for the conversion of the Sacristy of San Lorenzo into the Medici funeral chapel.

1521 Work begins on the Medici tombs in San Lorenzo.

1524 Beginning of the construction of the Laurentian Library. Designs are drawn up for the vestibule. Continuation of the figure ornamentation in the Medici Chapel, *Dusk*, *Dawn*; begins the figure of Lorenzo de' Medici.

1527 Fall of the Medici in Florence; during the turmoil *David* is damaged. The works in San Lorenzo come to a standstill.

1528 Michelangelo's favorite brother Buonarroto dies of the plague in July.

1529 Michelangelo becomes a member of the Defense Council of Nine and governor and procurator general of the Florentine Fortifications, for which he prepares many designs. In September he flees to Venice, suspecting betrayal by a commander of the Florentine city defenses.

1530 Continuing work on the Medici tombs. In August, the capitulation of the Florentine republic; after the return of the Medici, Michelangelo must hide, and the prior of San Lorenzo grants him protection. Marble sculpture of *David-Apollo*.

1531 Likely beginning of his association with Vittoria Colonna. Michelangelo's father Ludovico dies.

1532 Fourth version of contract for the Julius tomb. On a visit to Rome, he meets the Roman nobleman Tommaso de' Cavalieri.

1533 Drawings for Tommaso de' Cavalieri.

1534 Confirmation of the commission for *The Last Judgment* in the Sistine Chapel from Pope Paul III. Completion of the Medici tombs.

1535 Paul III appoints Michelangelo on September 1 as Supreme Architect, Sculptor, and Painter of the Apostolic Palace. Beginning of the works for *The Last Judgment* on the altar wall of the Sistine Chapel.

1538 Under commission from Cardinal Niccolò Ridolfi, he produces *Brutus* bust. Pope Paul III commissions Michelangelo to redesign the Piazza del Campidoglio.

Risen Christ, 1519–21. Marble, 80¾ in. (205 cm) high (without cross). Santa Maria sopra Minerva, Rome.

Culture

1524 Erasmus of Rotterdam attacks Luther in his *Discourse on Free Will*.

1527 Paracelsus publishes the foundations of his new medicine at Basel University.

1528 Count Baldassare Castiglione publishes his treatise on the ideal courtier, *Il Cortegiano*. Albrecht Dürer dies.

1529 Albrecht Altdorfer paints his most famous work, *The Battle of Alexander*.

1530 Correggio, the precursor of Italian Baroque painting, finishes his most famous fresco, the *Assumption of the Virgin*, in Parma Cathedral.

1532 Hans Holbein the Younger emigrates to England. *Portrait of the Merchant Georg Gisze* becomes one of his most famous works.

1534 Francesco Guicciardini writes his *Storia d'Italia*, the first history of Italy based on sources. Luther's complete translation of the Bible appears in Wittenberg. Ignatius of Loyola founds the Society of Jesus.

1535 Giulio Romano paints the ceiling frescoes in the Palazzo del Tè in Mantua. The English statesman Thomas More is beheaded for refusing to swear allegiance to Henry VIII as head of the Anglican Church.

1538 Vittoria Colonna's poems are published.

Titian, *Venus of Urbino*, ca. 1538. Oil on canvas, 46¾ x 65 in. (119 x 165 cm). Uffizi Gallery, Florence.

1541 Death of Rosso Fiorentino, who introduced Italian Mannerism to France, and had been working on the fresco painting in the palace of Fontainebleau.

1542 The architect Andrea Palladio completes the Godi Valmarana villa in Lonedo (Vicenza).

1545 Agnolo Bronzino, court painter of the Medici, executes frescoes in the chapel of Eleonore of Toledo, wife of Duke Cosimo I. The first botanical garden in Europe is created in Padua.

1546 Building work begins on the Louvre, city palace of the French kings. Martin Luther dies.

History

Execution of rebellious peasants, print from a contemporaneous drawing.

Adrian VI (1522–23). The Edict of Worms proscribes Luther as a heretic.

1523 Pope Clement VII succeeds Adrian VI (Giulio de' Medici, until 1534).

1524 Beginning of the German Peasants' War: The peasants rise up against the authorities and set out their demands in the "Twelve articles."

1525 Battle of Pavia. In the greatest battle of the century, Charles V defeats the French King Francis I.

1527 The Sack of Rome by mercenaries of Charles V's army. Clement VII escapes to Castel Sant'Angelo.

1529 Peace of the Ladies at Cambrai, so called because it was negotiated by Louise of Savoie and Margaret of Austria, ends the second Franco-Habsburg war between Francis I of France and Charles V. Siege of Vienna by Sultan Suleiman II.

1530 Pope Clement VII crowns Charles V emperor in Bologna, the last imperial coronation in Italy by a pope.

1531 Founding of the Schmalkaldic League of Protestants. Henry VIII of England becomes head of the Anglican Church. The Spaniard Francisco Pizarro conquers the Inca empire.

1532 The Edict of Worms against Protestants is repealed by Charles V.

1534 Paul III (Alessandro Farnese, 1534–49) becomes pope. Murder of Alessandro de' Medici.

1542 The Inquisition gathers force in Italy under Pope Paul III (forms Congregation of the Holy Office of the Inquisition).

1545 The Council of Trent is opened; it is held in three sessions until 1563.

1546 Charles V begins the Schmalkaldic War; the emperor's troops defeat the Protestant Schmalkaldic League (until 1547).